Lilies

RHS WISLEY HANDBOOKS

Lilies

Michael Jefferson-Brown

CASSELL ILLUSTRATED

THE ROYAL HORTICULTURAL SOCIETY

First published in Great Britain in 2002 by
Cassell Illustrated
Octopus Publishing Group
2–4 Heron Quays, London E14 4PJ

A CIP catalogue record for this book is available
from the British Library
ISBN 0-304-36326-X

Art Editor: Justin Hunt
Designer: Martin Hendry
Commissioning Editor: Camilla Stoddart

Printed in Slovenia by DELO tiskarna
by arrangement with Prešernova družba

CONTENTS

Title Page:
Lilium longiflorum,
the Easter Lily, is a
species that is slightly
tender but makes a fine
pot plant and is much
used as a cut flower.

INTRODUCTION

The lily may become the most important decorative flower of the century. In the UK alone, over 200 million cut stems are sold each year, which ensures that we are all very conscious of their existence. Lilies for indoor display are for sale in florists' shops all year round in an interesting variety, and for the garden, modern hybrids grow very easily to give splendid results. At a time when gardens are shrinking to relatively small plots, lilies as potted plants can be used on patios or moved into prime sites in beds and borders, to brighten up a surprising number of months. The wide range of colours, forms, sizes and characters ensure that their appeal remains fresh.

As a hobby plant, the lily is welcomed by all kinds of gardeners: those with little time or energy can get spectacular results, the novice will find lilies the easiest of all bulbs in pots, and the specialist can build up a very wide-ranging collection. If a challenge is relished, there are a number of species that require extra vigilance and more tailor-made conditions. Propagation is often at the heart of gardening as a hobby, and here the lily scores heavily (see 'Propagation and Breeding', pp.44–55). Few plants can be propagated so successfully in so many ways and breeding new kinds of lily is not difficult.

WHAT IS A LILY?

While a large number of plants have 'lily' as part of their common name, such as lily-of-the-valley (*Convallaria*), daylily (*Hemerocallis*) and Guernsey lily (*Nerine sarniensis*), true lilies belong to the genus *Lilium*, which is in the Liliaceae family.

'Star Gazer' is an Oriental type lily which is a leading cut flower and pot plant but is also a splendid garden cultivar.

6

The giant lily (*Cardiocrinum*) was once classified as a true lily, but it has a different method of growing; sensibly, it is now given its own genus. See p.93 for a list of false lilies.

True lilies are all bulbous, herbaceous perennials. They have a swollen organ, known as a bulb, buried at or under the soil surface. Bulbs store the energy resources of the plant, so when the top-growth dies back during droughty summers or cold winters, it will be able to grow again the following season. The Madonna lily, *Lilium candidum*, is almost the only exception to this rule: although most of the top-growth dies back during 'dormancy', a ring of leaves remains above the ground through winter.

LILIES IN THE WILD

Lilium is a genus of the Northern Hemisphere, and there are between 80 and 100 species spread over Europe, Asia and North America, most of which are plants of scrub or mountainsides.

Lilium candidum, the Madonna lily, has been associated with human civilization from well before the Christian era. It remains one of the best loved garden lilies.

Some species are confined to small pockets, while others can range over huge areas, as does *L. martagon*, which is known from Siberia to the Balkans and across southern Europe. Sometimes it is difficult for botanists to establish the true home of a species. For example, the Madonna lily, *L. candidum*, was associated with religion before the Christian era and was planted widely as food and decorative plant beyond its native haunts; as a result, its true origin is obscure.

Lilies have long suffered from being too showy for their own good, and in the past they were collected indiscriminately from the wild. Nowadays, there are many wild lilies under threat as agriculture becomes even more mechanized, land under cultivation expands, and buildings and roads take over wide tracts. The problem is compounded by the fact that all parts of the lily are edible to many grazing animals.

A BRIEF HISTORY OF LILIES

Bulbs are handy plants to transport, and as a result, many kinds of lilies were introduced into gardens from early times. *Lilium candidum* and *L. martagon* were two early entries. Further species, which initially found their way to bulb growers in Holland, quickly came to Britain, and as European plant explorers travelled further afield, Asian and American lilies began to be discovered. China and Japan began to yield up their treasures from the second half of the nineteenth century into the twentieth century with the introduction of *L. regale* and *L. auratum*, which were highlights of these exciting times. During this period, some of the lilies being cultivated were natural hybrids from the wild, or were hybrids that had occurred in gardens when species were brought close together, often for the very first time. These provided a range of plants for gardeners and were grown under the labels *L. × hollandicum*, *L. umbellatum* and similar names, and they were the first of the Asiatic hybrids. Some unusual hybrids also came about, such as *L. × testaceum* from a cross between the Madonna lily, *L. candidum*, and *L. chalcedonicum*.

Purposeful hybridization began in the twentieth century. By the 1920s, a number of useful Asiatic and Trumpet kinds were being offered to gardeners, but it was Jan de Graaff's work in Oregon that awoke the world to the fact that many new races of garden-worthy lilies were awaiting their attention. He gathered together as many species and hybrids as he could and with a dedicated band of helpers, he crossed huge numbers of flowers. The genus was given a huge boost as a garden plant when his Oregon Bulb Farms introduced the results of the breeding work from the middle of the last century onwards. Asiatic hybrids like 'Enchantment' are still first-rate garden plants, and some of the Trumpet hybrids, such as the Pink Perfection, African Queen and Golden Splendour Groups, are still leading types.

It soon became apparent that many Asiatic hybrids made excellent cut flowers, and an industry devoted to growing these plants by the million established itself. The easiest cut flowers to pack and handle were the upright-facing ones, and it is for this reason that breeders have tended to concentrate on these types.

ANATOMY OF A LILY

The bulbs

Bulbs are a type of underground bud consisting of tightly packed and overlapping, fleshy scales. They vary in size and shape, and are used by plants to store food. Lily bulbs may be white, cream, yellow or purple, and many are naturally pale in the soil, becoming coloured when exposed to the air. They also vary in shape, from round to disc-shaped (wider than they are deep) or narrower ones (deeper than they are wide). The nose (or noses) is the top part of the bulb where the growing shoot may be expected to grow through. As the bulbs start into

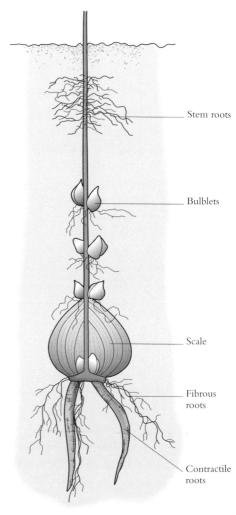

Most widespread method of growth showing a concentric bulb with bulblets and stem roots.

Stem roots

Bulblets

Scale

Fibrous roots

Contractile roots

growth, the nose becomes more prominent.

Roots grow from the base, or basal plate, of the bulb. When the stems have emerged above ground, the majority of lilies also grow a series of 'stem roots' in informal rings around the stem, between the bulb and the soil surface. These stem roots can be very energetic and perform two roles: they anchor the stem firmly in the soil and supplement the feeding activity of the basal roots.

Lilies have four different bulb forms called concentric, rhizomatous, stoloniferous and stoloniform, which are described below, with the most common first.

Concentric bulbs

These are formed of a number of scales that more or less overlap one another. Concentric lily bulbs have a central growing point in a similar manner to daffodil or onion bulbs, but they do not have successive layers of unbroken scales like Russian dolls. In some, such as *Lilium monadelphum* and *L. martagon*, the scales are numerous and narrow. The scales of *L. martagon* are waisted or jointed and can be easily broken

Concentric bulb is the most usual bulb form.

across into halves. Concentric bulbs can vary in size from about 2cm (¾in) in diameter for a mature bulb of *L. concolor*, to over 20cm (8in) across in some of the Trumpet or Oriental hybrids.

Rhizomatous bulbs

In some species, the growing point or points tend to move sideways with the scales arranged more loosely around the basal parts. *Lilium pardalinum* is the best example of this type. Each season, as an old stem dies down, one or two new buds will form on the bulb ready to become the launching pads for next year's stems. Eventually, a considerable mass of scaly growth will be formed, like a rough mat with growing points around the perimeter. Older parts may take a considerable number of seasons to die away. One or two species are more upright like concentric bulbs, but they lurch somewhat sideways when developing new growth points. These are termed subrhizomatous bulbs. Rhizomatous bulbs can make a mat well over 30cm (12in) across.

Rhizomatous bulbs expand sideways.

Stoloniferous and stoloniform bulbs

A few lily bulbs, such as those of *Lilium canadense*, are known as stoloniferous bulbs. They send out thick stems sideways from the parent bulb, with new bulbs forming at the ends of these shoots or stolons. Stoloniform bulbs are seen in a small number of lilies. These are like traditional concentric bulbs, but the shoot that emerges from the bulb wanders around a while before making for the surface and proceeding to raise a stem. At intervals along this wandering subterranean stem, a number of new bulbs are armed. *L. nepalense* and *L. duchartrei* have stoloniform bulbs and behave in this way.

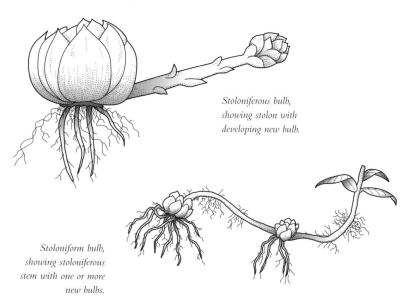

Stoloniferous bulb, showing stolon with developing new bulb.

Stoloniform bulb, showing stoloniferous stem with one or more new bulbs.

The leaves

Lily leaf forms vary around three basic shapes: narrowly linear, elliptical, or pointed with the widest part of the leaf at the stem end. The leaves are arranged alternately or scattered along the stems, sometimes in prolific numbers; in some, the stems are left bare between whorls of leaves. This whorled arrangement is typical of *Lilium martagon* and many North American species, such as *L. pardalinum*. Some leaves tend to clasp the stems and others point at angles from them, varying between the vertical and horizontal. Most are glossy and gently arch along their length. While the vast majority have leaves that abut the stems, some, such as the leaves of *L. speciosum*, have stalks. The first leaf of the majority of lilies, the cotyledon or seed leaf, will be a narrow strap; the next leaf will be the first true leaf, elliptical in shape.

Leaves scattered and tending to clasp stem.

Leaves horizontal and alternate.

Leaves arranged in separate whorls.

The flowers

All lily flowers are formed of six 'petals', although the three outer ones seen when the flower is in bud are really sepals. These three sepals may be more or less identical to the three true petals within, but the sepals may be broader. In lilies like *Lilium regale*, the sepals may be coloured quite strongly on the outside surface, unlike the petals. Botanically, petals and sepals are collectively known as the perianth, but for simplicity, the term 'petals' shall be used in this book.

Plants of the closely related daffodil family (Amaryllidaceae) are clearly distinct from those of the lily family (Liliaceae) in having flowers with petals that enclose only the anthers and stigma; the ovary sits *behind* the point where the petals attach themselves to the flower. Lilies have petals that enclose all sexual parts, with the ovary sitting *in front of* the point of petal attachment. The ovary can produce a large number of seeds, perhaps over 100.

The petals of lilies are variably curved, giving rise to the different flower forms. Rarely, the petals are concave and form a globe as in *L. mackliniae*. Sometimes, they point outwards to form a wide bowl or a star shape, and there are many examples in which the petals curl backwards nearly making a cylinder, almost like a ball as in *L. martagon*. These are often described as 'turk's caps', a rather out-dated term.

Each petal has a longitudinal furrow down the centre; these are often a green colour and give a central green star effect. The furrows point to the nectary in the middle of the flower. Around the nectary, and maybe advancing to the centre of each petal, there can be a series of raised, pimple-like spots, known as papillae. The roughness this causes on the petals is noticeable in several important species and their hybrid offspring. *L. speciosum* is well endowed with papillae and *L. henryi* can be spectacularly so.

In most lilies, the anthers are relatively large. In Trumpet hybrids, they can be as much as 3cm (1¼in) long. Anthers can form a significant decorative part of the flower, with the pollen colour usually a rich, rusty orange. Fresh pollen is somewhat sticky and can stain skin, clothes or furniture. Loose pollen can be blown off skin and fabric; flicking the underside of the

Lilium speciosum var. rubrum is a Japanese species of Oriental group, one of the founder species of the brilliant Oriental hybrids.

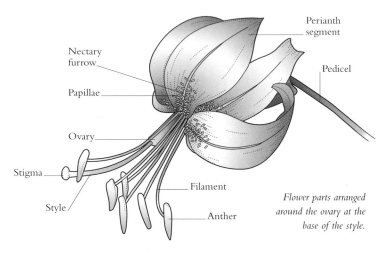

Nectary furrow

Papillae

Ovary

Stigma

Style

Perianth segment

Pedicel

Filament

Anther

Flower parts arranged around the ovary at the base of the style.

material can dislodge larger amounts. The remaining pollen should be allowed to dry before being brushed away. Trying to wipe away fresh pollen is likely to ensure an awkward stain.

Lily flowers may be arranged singly on the stem, or borne in heads or clusters of up to 150. Flower stalks, or pedicels, have a considerable impact on the character of the flowerheads. Sometimes the pedicels are short, as in some upright Asiatic hybrids, and the flowers can be crowded as a result. *Lilium martagon* has rather limited pedicels, so the flowers are held stiffly to make narrow columns of blossom. Species like *L. speciosum* and *L. canadense* have notably long flower stalks, and this enables the blooms to be displayed in a more airy and graceful manner. Among the lilies, flower pose ranges from upward-facing sky-worshippers through every angle to severely pendent.

Fragrance is not universal in lilies; the trumpets and the orientals are very generously endowed but most of the Asiatic hybrids and their ancestor species are not perfumed or have only a very slight suggestion. This may change as one or two of the newer Asiatics have some scent.

CLASSIFICATION OF LILIES

Lilies are classified as either species or garden types. Beyond these two basic definitions lie many smaller units of classification. The species lilies, for example, include all the true species, and they are usually split into seven groups:

1. Martagon
2. American
3. Candidum
4. Oriental
5. Asian
6. Trumpet
7. Dauricum

The main characteristics that differentiate the seven wild lily groups are listed as follows, in order of importance: method of seed germination; arrangement of leaves; entire or jointed bulb scales; heavy or light seed; bulb form and habit; petals smooth or with papillae; nectary with or without hairs; turk's-cap or trumpet flower shape; white or purple bulb, stem erect or stoloniform; obvious or absent/obscure leaf stalks; large or small stigma; stem-rooting or not stem-rooting; and one or more stems per bulb.

Main types of hybrid lilies

The classification of hybrid or garden lilies tries to echo that of the wild lily groups. Hybrid lilies are also split into seven divisions, but there are distinct differences. While this classification attempts to impose some order on the huge number of hybrids, a perfect classification system is becoming more and more difficult to establish as a result of wider interbreeding. Species lilies are sometimes classified separately, as Division IX.

Main types of garden lilies

At present, three types of hybrids dominate the lily world: the Asiatics, the Trumpets and the Orientals. They complement each other with the flowers of the Asiatics opening first, usually in early summer, the Trumpets coming a little later, possibly in mid- and late summer, and the Orientals overlapping, but with later kinds reaching into early autumn. In pots, the bulbs can be persuaded to bloom at different times; it is easy to encourage earlier blooming, a little harder to delay them (see 'Lilies in Pots and Containers', p.25).

A typical Asiatic hybrid – such as 'Apollo', 'Connecticut King' or 'Enchantment' – will grow to about 80cm (32in) tall. Its stems will carry up to ten or more scentless flowers, which open in early summer and are still present through midsummer.

The Classification of Hybrid Lilies

Division	Description	Examples
I	**Asiatic hybrids** are derived from the crossing of species such as *L. amabile*, *L. bulbiferum*, *L. cernuum*, *L. concolor*, *L. davidii*, *L. dauricum*, *L. lancifolium*, *L. leichtlinii* and *L. pumilum*. Apart from the European *L. bulbiferum*, these are all Asian species, and so the cultivars are usually referred to as Asiatic hybrids. Bulbs are concentric, foliage is scattered, and flowers appear during early and midsummer. There are many cultivars. A new development has been the crossing of Asiatic hybrids with the trumpet species *L. longiflorum*; the resulting progeny are exceptionally strong plants with many large flowers and are often referred to as LA hybrids ('L' for *longiflorum* and 'A' for Asiatic).	
Ia	Cultivars with flowers that face upwards in umbels or racemes	'Apollo', 'Corina', 'Côte d'Azur', 'Enchantment', 'Grand Cru', 'Orange Pixie', 'Rodeo'
Ib	Cultivars with flowers that face outwards	'Fire King', 'King Pete'
Ic	Cultivars with flowers that face downwards	'Barbara North', Citronella Group
II	**Martagon-type hybrids** are usually the crossbred progeny of *L. martagon* and *L. hansonii*. Bulbs are concentric, usually with jointed scales, flowers are a turk's-cap shape, and foliage is whorled. There are a limited number, but they are very useful as garden plants.	*L.* × *dalhansonii* 'Marhan'
III	**Candidum hybrids** and hybrids from European species. These are derived from *L. candidum*, *L. chalcedonicum* and *L. monadelphum*. Bulbs are concentric, leaves are scattered, flowers usually face outwards or downwards. There are few cultivars.	*L.* × *testaceum* is virtually the only widely known member of this division

Division	Description	Examples
IV	**Hybrids of American species** are usually derived from *L. pardalinum*. Bulbs are often rhizomatous bulbs, foliage is whorled and flowers are usually pendent with recurved petals.	'Cherrywood'
V	**Longiflorum hybrids** are derived from *L. longiflorum* and *L. formosanum*. Bulbs are concentric, foliage is scattered, flowers are trumpet-shaped. There are very few cultivars.	'White American'
VI	**Trumpet hybrids** are derived from trumpet species and may involve *L. henryi* or its hybrids. Bulbs are concentric with large scales, and foliage is scattered. There are many cultivars.	
VIa	Cultivars with trumpet-shaped flowers	African Queen Group, Pink Perfection Group
VIb	Cultivars with bowl-shaped flowers	'Lady Ann'
VIc	Cultivars with flat flowers	'Bright Star'
VId	Cultivars with distinctly recurved flowers	'Lady Bowes Lyon'
VII	**Oriental hybrids** are derived from Far-Eastern species, such as *L. auratum*, *L. speciosum* plus any hybrids of these with *L. henryi*. Bulbs are concentric, foliage is scattered or alternate, leaves are usually stalked. There are many cultivars.	
VIIa	Cultivars with trumpet-shaped flowers	'Sam' (syn. 'Mr Sam')
VIIb	Cultivars with bowl-shaped flowers	'Casa Blanca'
VIIc	Cultivars with flat flowers	'Star Gazer'
VIId	Cultivars with recurved flowers	'Acapulco', 'Black Beauty', 'Journey's End'

For growers interested in propagating lilies, a large Asiatic bulb will usually split into two after blooming, and there are likely to be a few bulblets (immature bulbs) clustered on that part of the stem in the soil; some cultivars may produce bulbils in the leaf axils. The Trumpet hybrids are usually taller with 10 to 30 fragrant flowers; stems of Pink Perfection Group may reach 2m (6ft) tall. They have large bulbs, which increase steadily rather than dramatically, and they can produce bulblets but bulbils are rarely seen in the leaf axils. Oriental hybrids like 'Star Gazer', 'Mona Lisa' and 'Casa Blanca' are highly fragrant with large, open flowers. Their bulbs may provide bulblets, and the outer scales may be fostering a small new bulb. Traditional Oriental hybrids are lime-haters and will not tolerate alkaline soils. Plant them in soils with a pH of 6.5 or below, or in an ericaceous (lime-free) compost.

TODAY AND THE FUTURE

Lilium is a dynamic genus made even more so by the dedicated work of plant breeders. A major breakthrough was the mating

'Enchantment' is a famous Asiatic cultivar introduced in the 1950s and still widely grown as a cut flower and garden plant.

of Trumpet hybrids with *Lilium henryi*, an orange-flowered species with recurved petals. The importance of this alliance was the variety of flower forms that resulted, and all offspring with *L. henryi* blood seem to inherit its indifference to lime. Relatively recently, these plants and their parent species were mated with Oriental hybrids to produce a new race

'Conneticut King' is an Asiatic lily, bred originally as a spotless, golden cut-flower, this also does well in the garden.

of lime-tolerant Orientals, sometimes listed as Orienpets. Most widely grown of these is 'Black Beauty', which is capable of producing stems that carry 50–150 crimson blooms. As these types become more widely distributed, their immense garden value is going to be realized.

The other revolutionary advance is the mating of the Easter lily, *L. longiflorum*, with various Asiatic hybrids. In Britain, the Easter lily is usually grown as a greenhouse plant as it is on the borderline of hardiness. No such taunt can be levelled at the offspring, sometimes listed as LA hybrids. They are hugely vigorous and hardy, with the bulbs increasing quickly and producing large heads of flowers, from 10–30 on ramrod stems. It could be that these will supersede the traditional Asiatics in time. We shall see.

WHERE TO GROW LILIES

There can be few spots in temperate regions like Britain where lilies cannot be grown. Most gardens can support a wide selection. There are a few kinds, however, that will only succeed outside in milder regions, such as south-west England, and it would be risky to grow them outside elsewhere. An example would be the Easter lily, *Lilium longiflorum*. Some species demand the perfect environment, but the inhibitions of many of these have vanished in the hybrid offspring. Finally, there are species that do better in different regions: *L. mackliniae*, for example, is certainly easier to please in gardens in Scotland and northern England than it is in southern ones.

SITE AND SHADE

Lilies are not shrinking violets; they are major stars rather than bit-players and make a considerable impact wherever they bloom. Stars sometimes need careful handling and we must match each to its setting. What looks splendid on the patio can be almost grotesque in between shrubs or in light woodland, and some of the upright Asiatic hybrids can look really out of place in a wild setting. A few bulbs can certainly bring life to a scene that threatens to be dull, but by the house we expect one type of performance, at a distance we need another.

The range of lily species and cultivars is tremendous, so there is usually a wide selection for every type of garden venue. All we need to be sure of is that there is enough light and that the soil, ideally neutral or slightly acid, is properly drained (see 'Sites and Soils', p.31). Good drainage is imperative, but beyond

'Snowstar', an Asiatic cultivar which has a free-flowering disposition and a generous attitude to bulb increase.

this there are few rules that cannot be broken. While choice of lily for patio containers probably means giving dwarf kinds prior claims, there may be places where head-high cultivars will be perfectly all right.

Where lilies are to remain *in situ* for decades, the planting choice will be more limited. We look first to the species that have evolved in the wild in natural conditions. There are kinds that can be left for years, decades, or forever. There are also a number of hybrids closely related to the species that will be equally good or even more successful. 'Cherrywood', a seedling

Lilium martagon *forms growing as if wild. They can be successfully left to do their own thing for decades.*

from the North American species *Lilium pardalinum*, has much of the character of the wild plant but is perhaps even stronger in growth and more decorative in its red and golden bloom. Citronella Group is a set of clones that can have a similar dainty effect, this time in deep lemon yellow shades; they have similarly pendent blooms with recurved petals. The group escapes the over-bred look of some modern garden flowers, retaining the natural refinement of the three species that are not far back in their breeding.

Deep woodland conditions will not suit lilies. They want to enjoy sun and light. However, a number will be very happy on the edge of woodland or in lightly shaded areas. The most satisfactory for these areas tend to be *L. martagon*, *L. hansonii*, *L. henryi*, *L. pardalinum*, and the hybrids derived from these species. Trumpet hybrids, *L. henryi*, and the new Orienpet hybrids, which are derived from the interbreeding of Oriental hybrids with *L. henryi*, can also be successful in lightly shaded areas on a long term basis.

LILIES IN POTS AND CONTAINERS

It is difficult to over-emphasize the importance of lilies in pots and other containers. This is often the way in which newcomers first grow lilies; a happy introduction, as lilies are the best of all bulbs in pots. The smaller the garden, the more useful potted lilies become, because they can be brought forward into prominence when in bud, and then relegated to a screened corner after flowering. More and more garden centres are offering such potted lilies ready to slip into place. The instant garden has nearly arrived!

While paved or gravelled places are usually thought of as the staging posts for flowering pots, container-grown lilies might also become focal points in beds or borders where colour and interest are needed. Because of the widespread interest in growing lilies in containers, this method of culture is given careful attention in the next chapter. Anyone who has tried them will agree that lilies are wonderfully responsive to life in a container.

Under the glass of a cool greenhouse or conservatory, lily bulbs planted in autumn can be brought into bloom one or two months before their normal time without resorting to artificial heat. They will do well under glass at any time, but they need some respite from the excessive heat possible during summer. Otherwise, their display will come and go in a day or two rather than last a few weeks.

Several sets of dwarf lilies are very suitable for patio pots. The Pixie Series covers most colours; they are very easy Asiatic hybrids growing between 30–50cm (12–20in) tall. There are also an increasing number of Oriental hybrids, such as 'Mona Lisa', that grow within the same limits. Another group marketed as Kiss Lily Series, 45–50cm (18–20in) tall, are so called because they have no pollen – they can be handled without fear of pollen marks. They grow as easily as any others and sometimes have extra petals in place of the anthers; 'White Kiss' and the dusty pink 'Little Kiss' are two examples. All Asiatic hybrids except very tall ones are suitable for pots, as are the species *L. longiflorum*, *L. regale* and *L. speciosum*.

If anyone should wish to do so, it would be possible to have pots of lilies in bloom from mid-spring until early autumn without involving any unusual routines. To achieve this, pick cultivars that bloom naturally at different times. The earlier ones can be potted in good time and given a little extra warmth to encourage even more precocious flowers. If you want a particular cultivar to be delayed, the bulbs can be stored in a refrigerator for weeks or even months before potting and then kept fairly cool, which results in blossom several weeks later than normal. Early lilies include 'Red Carpet', 'Fire King' and *L. bulbiferum*. Late-flowering lilies include *L. speciosum* and 'Journey's End'.

LILIES IN BEDS AND BORDERS

Special beds for lilies have been popular in the past, but nowadays it is more usual to integrate the bulbs with herbaceous plants and shrubs, a method which has several advantages. First of all, lilies like to have their faces in the sun and their toes in the shade. This is easily managed in the mixed border or shubbery. Secondly, as the new shoots of lilies break through the soil in spring and begin to grow, they can be vulnerable to frost. Surrounding vegetation will help to

'Mona Lisa' is a dwarf Oriental division cultivar with large perfumed blooms. Good in pots or towards the front of the border.

deflect the frost. Thirdly, the stems of wild lilies often need the support of shrubs they are growing through; this sort of neighbourly assistance may be helpful to species like *L. henryi* and *L. davidii*, which often have stems that grow at an angle. Lily hybrids rarely need this support. The final advantage to growing lilies in a mixed border is that the surrounding plants can help mark the spot where lily bulbs lie dormant below the soil and labels have been lost or moved.

If the growth of nearby plants is too dense, however, it may preclude the free movement of air. This is unhelpful and can encourage the fungus *Botrytis*. While there is a lot to be gained from neighbouring plants, too intrusive familiarity can be a little dangerous. Despite this, there are many occasions when the colour and form of flowering lilies can be greatly enhanced by a background of foreign foliage. One has to use some judgement about how close to a shrub to plant bulbs; shrubs can grow with surprising speed, and in two or three years they could have overgrown the lilies, threatening their health or even their lives. Most Asiatic hybrids are best lifted every two or three years to prevent overcrowding and to check their health. Following such a regime will minimize the danger of suffocation.

A single lily can look lovely, but three or more planted as a group will look far more than three times as good. There is some magic arithmetic that conjures up this extra beauty. This means that one needs space enough for at least three fully grown lilies, and preferably enough space to allow for some increase if they are to be left *in situ* for more than one season.

NATURALIZED LILIES

There is something most appealing about bulbs that can be planted and left alone to increase in number and effectiveness year by year. They look happy and have a sense of being properly at home. This can happen with a number of lilies, often species and their closely related hybrids. Planning to naturalize lilies is not foolhardy. Both *L. martagon* and *L. pyrenaicum*, originally from southern Europe to Asia and the Pyrenees respectively, have gone walkabout and established themselves in the wild in a few places in Britain. There are

'Black Beauty' is one of a new race of Oriental lilies that are tolerant of lime. An exceptionally strong and beautifully floriferous plant.

gardens where *L. martagon* has been growing from between 50 and 100 years or more.

Other lilies particularly recommended for naturalizing include *L. lancifolium*, *L. candidum*, *L. pardalinum*, *L. henryi*, and 'Cherrywood'. The last three, as well as *L. martagon*, are notably reliable and long-lasting. Where *L. pardalinum* or *L. martagon* and its hybrids have been planted with a long-term tenancy in mind, the dangers of encroaching trees and shrubs can be more

Lilium martagon *var.* album.
White forms of the martagon lily can be spotted or pure white, and are prized as a contrast to the coloured forms.

serious, but their company should not be shunned, as these lilies can look enchanting in light woodland conditions. Avoid planting under dense canopies or very close to trees, and all should be well.

Lilies with graceful, pendent flowerheads, such as *L. martagon*, *L. pardalinum*, and their close relatives, seem to appear more at home between trees than the more formal hybrids. This applies equally to both deciduous trees, like silver birches, and to evergreen conifers. If thinking in terms of Asiatic hybrids, then it would be the nodding heads of the Citronella Group or the dainty hybrids bred by Dr M. North that may be the most effective in such situations. One of the most natural of associations is that of rhododendrons with lilies. Rhododendron shrubs will only flourish in an acid soil, and this will certainly suit most lilies. They will be sheltered by the evergreen shrubs, which will also provide a dark backdrop for the lily flowers. The bulbs will be afforded protection and be kept at an even temperature.

The species *L. martagon* and *L. szovitsianum* are capable of increasing their territory by seed once their bulbs have established themselves and if the seedlings are left undisturbed. Such seedlings may take several years to reach flowering size – in some cases, as long as seven years. The same seed, if gathered and sown under controlled conditions, can produce mature lilies in half the time.

Sites and soils

There are lilies capable of growing outside in all parts of the British Isles. Cold winters are not necessarily an obstacle. Winter wet is the problem, one that may be aggravated by cold temperatures. Poorly drained soils must be avoided. When 'good drainage' is recommended, which is what lilies enjoy, an open soil that is full of air is being advocated. It should not be liable to waterlogging. To encourage an open soil structure, incorporate plenty of well-rotted organic matter into the soil, such as leafmould, peat or well-rotted garden compost.

Lilies do not need a lot of water through winter, therefore it is best to keep them fairly dry, not desiccated, but moist rather than wet. The wild species lilies are often covered with a thick blanket of insulating snow, which keeps the soil from getting saturated and can prevent freezing. Snow-covered soils in Canada have registered a temperature of 1°C (34°F) just 2.5cm (1in) below the surface when above the snow it was -30°C (-22°F).

Once growth has started in the early part of the year, an increasing amount of moisture is helpful; the equivalent of the snow melting on the mountainsides and the water moving through the stony soil. Anything that can be done to simulate these natural conditions will be beneficial, although it is certainly unwise to encourage precocious growth outdoors.

The majority of lilies grow happily in a neutral to slightly acid soil, and many types will even tolerate a little lime. It is the Oriental hybrids derived from the lime-hating species *L. auratum* and *L. speciosum* that are very sensitive to lime. For these lilies, lime can prove fatal, and they have to be grown in pots of lime-free (ericaceous) compost in gardens with limy (alkaline) soils. While slight alkalinity in the soil can be overcome by heavy additions of organic matter, moving the pH value just one point towards acid by such means is a mammoth task. One is best advised to take the long view and repeatedly top-dress with compost and leafmould year after year.

Many of today's Asiatic and Trumpet hybrids can tolerate a certain amount of alkalinity, especially if the soil is enriched with organic matter. *L. henryi* is often happier in alkaline soils. *L. martagon* and *L. hansonii* seem indifferent to low lime levels.

It must be emphasized that drainage is the first essential for successful lily culture. Some sites are naturally better drained than others, and the poorer ones can be modified by adding organic matter and horticultural grit, as well as providing drainage channels to lower areas, if necessary. Sloping ground, for example, may or may not be well drained, but at least the higher portions can be improved so excess moisture can drain to lower levels. Only one or two exceptional lilies will manage, on occasion, in what look like impossible conditions. A magnificent clump of ever-expanding *L. pardalinum* var. *giganteum* once grew in my father's garden in unmitigated orange London clay where rainwater would often hang around for days.

As mentioned previously, another very important environmental factor is the provision of adequate light and air movement. While some lilies will do well in light shade, heavy shade weakens and eventually kills the plants. Such plants can become prey to *Botrytis* which further hastens their decline.

Ideally, a site should not only be cleared of weeds, but also of pests before planting. As a pest, rabbits can wreak havoc; they eat all parts of the lily plant and are especially fond of the asparagus-like, newly emerged shoot tips. One can admire a mole's industry but despair of the results. To reduce the numbers of smaller pests, such as slugs and snails, a lot can be done by clean cultivation. A serious grower might dig the chosen sites thoroughly and keep them free of weeds for some months before planting, which will minimize the number of these and other pests. Please refer to the chapter dealing with pests (see p.56).

Lilium ×
dalhansonii
'Marhan' is over
a hundred years
old, a Martagon
division lily that
is marvellously
persistent and
trustworthy.

ASSOCIATED PLANTS

Lilies are gregarious. They look better with companions, especially if these have their own seasons of interest when the lilies are out of bloom. Shrubs of all kinds, barring the most rapacious growers, are natural allies. Many herbaceous plants also mix well, and those with differing growth and flowering habits to lilies are particularly attractive. It would be a mistake to plant lilies close to clumps of day lilies (*Hemerocallis*), as they bloom at the same time with flowers that resemble those of the lilies. Japanese anemones (*Anemone* × *hybrida*) would be better as they have contrasting foliage and come into bloom after the lilies have finished. If there are neighbouring clumps of daffodils (*Narcissus*), these will pay the rent in spring, and as their foliage dies away it can be masked by the growth of annuals like cornflowers (*Centaurea cyanus*), love-in-the-mist (*Nigella damascena*) and candytuft (*Iberis*). Their colours will often provide a pleasing, non-dominant contrast to the lilies. Hardy geraniums can also be very friendly neighbours; *Geranium macrorrhizum*, with its magenta flowers, can be a striking duo with pale Asiatic hybrids like 'Mont Blanc', 'Apollo' or 'Medaillon'. Many other geraniums could also be happy lily associates, especially those that take on pleasing autumn leaf colour when the lilies have died away or are merely seed stems. A very safe and pleasing association is lilies and ferns. The flowering stems look well with the fronds of the ferns below them, and evergreen ferns will help to protect the young lily shoots from frost. The contrast between lily foliage and that of ferns is also pleasing. Another possible contrast is that provided by the dark sculptural masses of bear's breeches (*Acanthus*), which are often planted for their foliage rather than their ladders of hooded flowers.

Lilies like companions. Here is a white Asiatic, 'Mont Blanc', with pink buds growing with Geranium macrorrhizum, *a good ground-covering species.*

How to grow lilies

Purchasing bulbs

There are plenty of lily bulbs available for sale either through garden centres or by mail order. You should be safe buying by mail order from catalogues, as firms will be jealous of their reputations and expect to build up goodwill so that repeat orders follow. Bulbs will be checked before they are sent out at a suitable time; the packaging will keep the goods intact. Unpack and plant the bulbs as soon as possible on receipt. If delay is unavoidable, bulbs are best kept just moist in peat or peat substitute – do not store them in airless plastic bags. If received in winter, they can be potted up and planted out *en bloc* in early spring.

Garden centres will display bulbs either loose in containers or in packets with illustrations. If you arrive soon after the loose bulbs have been put on display, they should be fresh and not in a dried-out state. The larger bulbs of a cultivar are going to perform better than the small ones. Look for plump, undamaged bulbs; they are vulnerable to bruising and may then start rotting. Extensive damage is going to invite disaster, but a small spot of blue penicillin mould is nothing to be worried about. The small, damaged spot can be soaked with fungicide and all should be well. An early arrival at a garden centre's tray of loose bulbs also reduces the risk of picking up a bulb that has been returned to the wrong place by a previous browser and finding a cuckoo in the nest at flowering time. It is often possible to get very good bulbs in this loose display arrangement, each one often significantly bigger than the same kind in a packet.

Lilium regale was found and introduced by the plant hunter Ernest Wilson as a very young man and it continues to be a very successful garden plant.

The same criteria apply when picking packets of bulbs, whether they are singletons, in threes or in other quantities. Avoid packets that have obviously been hanging around for a long time. It is possible to find bulbs that have completely dried out and are lifeless. Also avoid bulbs that have sprouted a few centimetres (inches), but if the stems have only just begun to emerge from the bulbs, they can be bought for immediate planting. Packets will normally be labelled with the cultivar name, the approximate height, flowering time, the flower colour and the specific lily type, such as Asiatic, Trumpet, Oriental or just 'species'. Sometimes, however, only a flower colour is specified. Bargain bags of mixed Asiatic or other hybrids are commonly offered. Although they are not expensive, they are best shunned as there is often no real clue as to the mix of flower colours included, and most gardeners like to know the names of their charges.

It is possible to raise your own bulbs by seed. There are seed firms who have a useful list of species and hybrid seed. See page 90 for seed and bulb sources and 'Propagation and Breeding' (pp.44–55) for details about raising seed.

WHEN TO PLANT

It is usually best to plant as soon as possible after purchase. If planting outside, this should be done in early autumn or early spring. The cold, wet winter is not going to encourage strong, healthy root growth.

Bulbs planted in early autumn will form a network of roots before winter, establishing an early relationship with the soil environment. This means that they will be better able to cope with the cold and wet of winter. The bulbs that are on sale in early spring will have been stored in controlled conditions so they are fresh and ready for action when bought. Introduced to the moisture and rising temperature of the soil in spring, bulb roots will get away to a sprint start, and growth should proceed quickly.

SOIL PREPARATION AND PLANTING

Choose a site that is naturally well drained, or arrange artificial drainage. The soil should be well dug and with plenty of

'Fiery Fred' is classified as an Asiatic but is one of the range of very strong hybrids between traditional Asiatic cultivars and Lilium longiflorum, cultivars sometimes listed as 'LA' hybrids.

organic matter added if possible; lilies are best with an open soil that is rich in air. It is still common practice for a handful of gritty sand to be placed below bulbs in the belief that drainage is thus improved. This is more likely to form a sump for water; the only possible benefit of this sand is that on lifting, bulbs may be shaken from the soil more easily.

Bulbs can then be tucked in at a depth that allows for a 10cm (4in) blanket of soil above their noses. In light, well-drained soils, the planting depth can be increased to give a 13–15cm (5–6in) covering above the bulbs. The planting distance between bulbs depends on the size of the fully grown plant. Most of the standard Asiatic hybrids should be happy separated by about 20cm (8in), but the Orientals need a little more elbow room. Larger Trumpet hybrids require at least 30cm (12in) of space between bulbs. If you want a more crowded effect, and the bulbs are going to be lifted after one season, it is possible to lessen the distances, but this would be very unwise if bulbs are to remain for two or more seasons. Gardeners hope for increase, but they rarely want something resembling a bamboo clump.

LILIES IN BORDERS

Lilies are star performers in borders. They will make much more impact if planted in groups of three or more, especially if a single cultivar is used, but a few groups of different kinds can be very exciting. They can often be left two or three years without lifting, some kinds even longer. While they will acquit themselves with distinction during their debut season, they should be noticeably better the following year. Then they may have more flowers per stem, and the stems will be higher. Trumpet hybrids can be at least 30cm (12in) higher in their second season.

It helps the plants to keep them

free of weeds. Although lilies benefit from the company of associated ornamental plants, this affection should not be of the smothering kind, which threatens the supply of light and air to the lilies.

CONTAINER CULTURE

Most gardeners will probably plant their first lilies in pots. They will be surprised how easily they grow and perform. Lilies are the best of all bulbs for pot culture. Planted in spring, the vast majority will be in bloom in about 100 days.

Provided there is adequate drainage, any sort of container can be used. The larger the container, the easier the culture, as soil temperatures and moisture content remain steadier. The smallest practical size for a single large bulb of a Trumpet hybrid or for three smaller Asiatic types will be a 20cm (8in) pot. The larger 25cm (10in) pots or half tubs are even better, with space for accompanying plants, even if they are only trailing lobelias or other modest annuals.

'Orange Pixie' is one of a series of dwarf Asiatics very well adapted to pot culture but also useful at the front of a border.

Oriental hybrids demand lime-free conditions, so use ericaceous potting composts. Incorporate some extra horticultural grit, which will be enjoyed by the roots, because of the more open soil structure. All other lilies can be grown in this type of potting compost. The only drawback of a soil-less, ericaceous potting mix is that it may prove difficult to get thoroughly wet again if it ever dries out. Lily growers often turn to John Innes No. 1 compost (a loam-based potting compost) instead, but add plenty of well-rotted organic matter, up to half as much again by volume. This certainly allows for easier watering, and the bulbs are tolerant of the small amount of lime introduced with the John Innes compost.

Potted bulbs can be kept under glass or in the open. Indoors, they are likely to grow more quickly, but they are perfectly safe outdoors and will not be damaged by cold unless a severe late frost catches the young shoots. Only a very prolonged, deep-reaching frost, probably of several days duration, is likely to damage the more-or-less dormant bulbs in pots in the depth of winter. To be safe, pots can be overwintered under bushes, or in a cool garage, conservatory, greenhouse or frame.

CARE IN GROWTH UNTIL FLOWERING

Apart from protection from a late frost when young shoots are just a few centimetres (inches) through the soil, there is not much to worry about until after flowering. Horticultural fleece or sheets of newspaper can give temporary frost protection, if necessary. In the open, natural watering will probably be more than adequate; potted lilies will dry out more quickly as the weather improves and the roots take out more water. Where convenient, potted lilies can be placed in a container of water and left until the surface becomes moist. This is a much more reliable method than watering from the top as pots may look wet when only the top inch or so is moist.

Most garden soils have enough nutrients to keep any lily happy, but plants can be given a boost by an early application of a general fertilizer, even though they do not demand it. High-nitrogen fertilizers are not a good idea; it is better to have potassium-rich types, such as those used for tomatoes, or a balanced fertilizer. Avoid getting fertilizer on the foliage.

Sometimes, it may be necessary to use stakes to support the stems as they grow. Bamboo stakes are usually unobtrusive, but inserting them into the ground may be hazardous; lilies frequently send up their flowering stems off-centre, so plunging a cane into the soil could bayonet the bulb. It is not possible to legislate for every contingency, but when planting, the ultra-cautious may wish to mark a cane position by inserting a small label or truncated cane by the side of any bulb likely to need later support. Alternatively, the soil around a growing bulb can be explored to establish its position before pushing in the stake.

'Roma' is taller and a little later to bloom than most Asiatics, a stately reliable lily.

In the spreading localities where lily beetles are active, the gardener must enter into combat. Occasionally, aphids may also be a nuisance. Battle plans are detailed in the 'Pests and Other Problems' chapter (see pp.56–63).

CARE AFTER FLOWERING

Most of the important work will have been done by the roots through the months up to and during flowering, but the longer we can promote healthy foliage and roots after flowering, the better the bulbs will do and the greater their increase. Unless you like to see the seedpods, or are aiming to collect seed, the flowering heads can be cut off after the flowers fail. No healthy leaves should be removed.

If potted lilies that have finished flowering are removed from their flowering quarters, it is then easy to forget them. But the bulbs will be better if watered regularly for a few more weeks. It may be that after a season in pots, the bulbs are going to be introduced into the open garden. This can be done when the plants have died down in early autumn or in early spring, or the whole pot can be tipped out immediately after flowering and planted *en bloc*. The bulbs should be at least 10–13cm (4–5in) deep in their new site.

LIFTING AND REPLANTING LILY BULBS

The best time to do this is in early autumn. The earlier flowering kinds will be easily managed, as they will have begun to go yellow in leaf, and the amount of active root work in the soil below will be minimal. Later kinds may be in full healthy leaf, but even these can be lifted before autumn is too advanced. The aim is to get the bulbs replanted before the cold winter weather arrives, and new roots will need to be produced well before this.

While Asiatic hybrids can have the old stems twisted off the bulbs, it is sensible to leave at least one-third or a half of the stem of Trumpet or Oriental hybrids when they are lifted for replanting. The shortened stems mark the position of the bulbs after replanting, even if they do not play much part in the overall health of the plant. The division of bulbs is dealt with in the next chapter.

PROPAGATION
AND BREEDING

The dynamism of the lily genus certainly extends to its means of propagation. Few other types of plant can boast so many easy methods of multiplication. Lily bulbs divide naturally like daffodils, and many produce bulblets on the stem between the top of the bulb and the soil surface. Bulbils can appear naturally in the leaf axils of some lilies and the traditional method of propagation that lily growers employ is to break off some scales from the parent bulb and getting these to produce bulblets. Finally, of course, there is nature's own way: by the prolific seed. It is common for a single pod to contain more than 100 viable seeds.

VEGETATIVE VERSUS SEED PROPAGATION

There are advantages to all the different methods of propagation, but there is a fundamental difference between growing new lilies from seed raising and all the other methods, which are all vegetative. Plants that arise from vegetative reproduction are grown from parts of the original plant; they are exact copies, carrying exactly the same genetic material and forming part of a single clone. Plants grown from seed are all individuals with their unique DNA or genetic material. Hybridization, the crossing of two distinct individuals, depends on sexual reproduction and the hybrid offspring have the potential to reflect charecteristics of both parents.

Clones are organisms with identical DNA. Separate identical cloned bulbs are really divided parts of one individual. If these clones happen to be a named kind, the convention is that this

Citronella Group. This pendent Asiatic group of clones are all dainty and worthy garden plants. Often a little taller than most Asiatics and with blooms arranged in a pyramid.

44

name be enclosed in quotes. 'Enchantment' would be an example.

If the clones are non-identical, but are raised from a similar parentage, then their names are not dignified with quotes. Such a collection of plants is termed a 'grex', although this is not a term that is commonly used by gardeners. Instead, the term 'strain' or 'group' is used. Citronella Group is an example.

The main advantages of vegetative propagation are ease, speed and the similar performance of offspring, since the offspring are exact copies of the parent. Flowers will match, plants will bloom at the same time, and they will grow in a similar fashion. There is one possible downside to vegetative propagation, however. If the original source plant is infected with a virus, it remains in the offspring. *Lilium lancifolium*, the tiger lily, is noted for the large number of bulbils it produces in its leaf axils, but it is also a species that is susceptible to virus infection. It is tempting to use the healthy looking bulbils when the plant is in fact diseased. Symptoms of the virus are not glaring; infected plants are marked with a series of paler stripes, but their metabolism is handicapped.

Lilies raised from seed will start free of viruses. Each new plant will also be a separate individual, with some new variation in character. Species pollinated with their own pollen will result in seeds bearing the characteristics of that species. Each of these seeds will grow into plants that clearly display the species character, but they may exhibit some subtle variation on the species character, which can take an almost infinite variety of forms. Perhaps it is in the overall vigour of the plant or in the size or average load of flowers. There may be a change in flower pigmentation; several lily species have yellow- and orange-flowered forms as well as pure whites. Some flowers can be heavily freckled, others with only a few beauty spots, and some completely free of this ornamentation.

Seed saved from cultivars will not reproduce their parents' looks. The mixed genetic inheritance can produce quite wide variations. If you know the breeding of the cultivar, it is usually possible to understand how the mixed brood have been produced. The more diverse the parentage, the wider the variation among the offspring. If a deliberate cross has been made between two distinct cultivars, a medley is guaranteed.

DIVISION OF LILY BULBS

A lily bulb flowers, then the flowering stem dies down and tends to divide the basal plate of the original bulb in two. Depending on the vigour of the plant and its age, this division will be more or less apparent. In time, the tissue between the two halves will perish and two independent bulbs function. When lily growers take the opportunity to split a dividing bulb, they crack open the divide by hand or plunge a knife down through the hole made where the defunct flower stem has been twisted away. The time to do this is in autumn, about eight weeks after flowering. On occasion, a bulb will have grown strongly and three or even more potentially independent bulbs will be obvious from the concentric rings of scales, and each can be carefully cut away from its neighbours. Before you replant divided bulbs, remove dead roots and any wasted tissue from former outer scales in order to examine the bulbs and make sure they are healthy. Small slugs and some damaged scales could be removed. Any physical damage will benefit from a 10-minute soak in a systemic fungicide solution before the bulb is replanted.

Rhizomatous bulbs may well benefit from being lifted and divided every two or three years, because they can form crowded mats of scales. The growing points are easily distinguished by the much paler colour of their scales. Lift these bulb mats gently and handle them carefully, as the scales are very brittle. Any scales that are detached can be used for propagation (see below). The rhizomatous mat can be severed with a sharp knife into pieces with at least one growing point each. The divisions are then replanted straight away, perhaps taking the opportunity of moving them to a fresh patch of soil or digging over the original site and enriching it with organic matter. Only very small divided bulbs will fail to bloom the year after planting.

PROPAGATION FROM SCALES

This popular method of reproduction could be viewed as an extension of bulb division. While it can be done at any time of year, the easiest time is very early spring so the resulting young plants can be grown on strongly through the warmer months ahead. Try to ensure that the bulb taken for propagation is free

Propagation from bulb scales

1 *Select healthy bulbs, avoiding any showing possible virus symptoms when in active growth.*

2 *Having removed any old wasted scales with collapsed tissue, break off plump scales as close to the bulb's basal plate as possible.*

3 *Soak scales in systemic fungicide according to maker's instructions (usually 15–20 minutes).*

4 Either *place soaked scales in clean plastic bag with moist Vermiculite or similar inert material. Seal the bag and place it in a light or dark environment at a temperature of 17–20°C (63–68°F).*

OR *insert scales into a tray of compost with the tips exposed. Place the tray into a bag, seal it and store it at a temperature of around 17–20°C (63–68°F).*

5 *After 6–8 weeks bulblets should be formed on fractured edge of each scale. If very tiny (3–4mm (1/8in) diameter), they can be left for 2–3 weeks more hoping for some fattening.*

6 *When bulblets are the size of peas, the bags can be opened. Bulblets can be broken from scales or left intact.*

7 *Bulblets or scales with bulblets are inserted in potting compost and grown on.*

of virus disease, something that can only be detected when the plant is in active growth and the leaves examined. The procedure is as illustrated.

When detaching scales, it is easiest to start with the outmost and work around the bulb as new ones are freed of their overlapping neighbours. Only use plump, healthy scales. The number of scales taken will depend on the size and health of the bulbs as well as the number of new bulbs desired. Between four and six taken from a good bulb should scarcely affect its vigour. A relatively small scale can be expected to provide at least one new bulblet, but larger ones may provide two or three or even more.

There are at least two ways to deal with the scales. One method is to place the fungicide-soaked scales in a plastic bag containing moist vermiculite or similar material to keep them damp, and then tying the bag with air enclosed. Label the bag with an indelible pen; one set of scales can look very like another. An indelible label could also be put inside the bag. Place the bag somewhere safe, in either light or dark conditions.

Another method is to insert the fungicide-soaked scales into labelled pots or trays of compost with the fractured margins of the scales under the compost and only their tips exposed. The compost may be half gritty sand and half peat or organic matter. Alternatively, you could use ericaceous compost. The compost should be moist but not sodden, and the pots or trays enclosed in polythene bags to ensure they do not dry out. They should be placed in a safe place, below greenhouse staging is a sensible position, and examined periodically.

Carefully detach the bulblets, which may have emerging roots, from each scale. Pot them up and cover with 2.5cm (1in) or more of potting compost. Alternatively, the whole scale may be potted up complete with all its bulblets. Whichever course is taken, keep the bulblets moist, treating them like adult bulbs. Three or more bulblets could be grown together for a while in a 10cm (4in) pot before being individually potted on. As the plants grow, they can be moved successively from 10cm (4in) to 13cm (5in) and 15cm (6in) pots. The best bet is to grow these plants for a whole season before planting out early the next spring. Well-grown bulblets may bloom in this second year.

In some parts of the world, lilies are propagated commercially by taking scales and placing them in shallow drills outdoors and growing them on. It is possible to do something similar in gardens, and it often happens inadvertently when handling bulbs of those like *L. martagon* and *L. pardalinum*, which have very brittle scales.

PROPAGATION FROM BULBLETS

Many lilies produce bulblets on the stem between the nose of the bulb and the soil surface. On occasion, some cultivars and species bear a dozen or more, but it is more usual to find four, five or six. Strong-growing plants, encouraged by fertile soil and plentiful moisture through the growing season, often yield more and larger bulblets. Bulblets vary in size from about 3mm (⅛in) across to nearly as big as a golf ball.

The bulblets are best separated from their parents and given room to grow without restriction. Lifting bulbs annually makes the collection of bulblets easy, but as an alternative to lifting, loosen the soil around the base of a stem and detach the stem and its bulblets from the bulb, perhaps by twisting. All bulblets can be grown on in the open or in containers in the same way as mature bulbs. Depending on their size, and assuming reasonable cultivation, the plants will bloom the year after planting or in the following season.

PROPAGATION FROM BULBILS

Bulbils are small bulbs that form in the axils of lily leaves. The best known lily to grow bulbils is the tiger lily, *L. lancifolium* (syn. *L. tigrinum*). A single stem of this species may bear anything from 12 to 100 bulbils. Some clones of the rarer yellow trumpet species *L. sargentiae* and the European species *L. bulbiferum* are also generous with bulbils. Hybrid lilies with these species in their background, a large number of Asiatic hybrids for example, will often inherit this easy means of increase. One or two bulbils per leaf axil is probably normal.

Bulbils may be very small, but they can grow as large as 2cm (¾in) or more in diameter. They can be vigorous and may start making root growth and even leaves while still firmly attached to the stem. If left to their own devices, the bulbils will eventually fall to the ground and make strong root growth. Contractile roots will have the ability to pull the young bulb down into the soil.

Non-flowering stems often bear a more prolific amount of bulbils. One way to ensure a useful number of bulbils is to sacrifice the flowering top of a plant at an early stage. When the small green flower buds are seen, cut the flowerhead away. If there is an inbred trait in a lily to develop bulbils, then this rather drastic treatment usually fully releases this inherent ability. The procedure for propagating lilies from bulbils is as follows:

Harvest bulbils approximately eight weeks after flowering or as soon as they are easily detached from the stem. This may mean taking one batch and then further lots as others swell and mature.

Plant bulbils in labelled pots or trays and grow on. They will certainly be safe in ericaceous potting compost, buried 2.5–6cm (1–2½in) deep. Those with little leaves can be allowed to wave their little green 'flags', but these will bury themselves deeper as the days and weeks pass until they are as deep as the leafless bulbils. Alternatively, bulbils can be grown in frames or even in the open ground if kept free of weeds.

In spring, the bulbs will be rooting and growing strongly. Pot them up individually and treat similarly to scale bulbils (see p.48). Large, early harvested bulbils have been known to bloom the following season if grown well. All bulbils should be capable of flowering in their second year.

Stem showing bulbils developing in leaf axils.

PROPAGATING BULBS FROM SEED

A lily seedpod may have just one to over 100 viable seeds, and each one is usually a rusty brown, flat disc. The embryo seedling with its root point can be seen if a bright light is shone through a seed. Unfertilized seeds form a light chaff, which can be separated from the viable seeds by being blown lightly. If left for a long time in a dry, warm spot, lily seeds lose their vitality. Seed can be sown immediately after harvest, or kept safe in a cool, dry place and sown in late winter. The safest place to store seed is in the domestic refrigerator, but not in the freezer compartment. On the whole, it is best to sow lily seeds immediately in pots and hope for a quick germination. Most lilies recommended in this book have seeds that grow quickly. The procedure is as follows:

Fill labelled pots or trays with ericaceous potting compost or with a neutral to slightly acid (ericaceous) seed compost, and scatter the seeds over the surface so that each is free of its neighbours. Cover them with only about 3mm (⅛in) of compost, grit or perlite.

Soak the seed containers in water until the surface of the compost is wet. Drain away any surplus water and then enclose the pots or trays in polythene bags or cling film.

Narrow seed leaves usually appear a few weeks after sowing. True leaves follow and when these have fully developed, or when each seedling has grown one or two more leaves, the young plants can be teased apart and potted individually. Asiatic and Trumpet hybrids can flower within 15 months from being sown; the white Trumpet species *L. longiflorum* can be brought into bloom in eight months. Vigorous hybrids and species are normally quick to flower, initially bearing single blooms with fuller heads the following seasons. Some, like *L. martagon*, are slow, taking from four to seven years to flower from germination, depending on how well they are grown.

Some lilies have seeds that germinate underground. The seeds produce tiny bulbs next to the seed case, and the bulbs start to root. Only some while later do the tiny bulbs declare their presence by producing a true leaf, not a seed leaf, above ground. Seeds of Oriental hybrids and many of the American species behave in this way. Their underground germination is triggered by relatively warm autumn weather, and they then need several weeks of winter cold before spring warmth encourages them to push up their little leaves. Oriental hybrids, North American species and their derivatives may be propagated from seed as follows:

Shake the seeds free of their pod and gently blow away any chaff. Introduce the seeds into a clean polythene bag along with sufficient amounts of moist vermiculite or similar material to keep the seed moist and not too crowded.

Tie the bag with a label inside, and also write the name of the plant and current date on the outside of the bag. Keep out of direct light, in a cupboard for example, at a temperature in the range of 18–23°C (64–73°F) for four to seven weeks. By this time the seed should have germinated and tiny bulbs formed.

Place the bag in the refrigerator for two months, having marked the bag with either the date of entry or the date two months later so that you remember when to take the germinated seeds out. This period simulates winter; the aim is to cool rather than freeze the germinated seed.

After two months, the tiny bulbs can be carefully removed one by one and introduced into potting compost in pots instead of shallow trays. The potting compost must be ericaceous for Oriental hybrids and is best if gritty and open. The little bulbs can be grown on under cool glass and moved into fresh pots as they get larger.

BREEDING NEW LILIES

The most encouraging thing about breeding lilies is that it is difficult to raise an ugly one. Professionals have concentrated on the upright-facing Asiatics, which are so useful for the very important cut-flower market, gardeners may find the outward-facing and pendent or partially pendent types even more appealing. Trumpet and Oriental hybrids, on the other hand, can produce lots of strong seed and this will give good seedlings. Lily cultivars will bear seed if pollinated by their own pollen, but they may be more prolific crossed with others of similar types.

The procedure is simple. Nip off the anthers with fingers or tweezers as the flower buds open and before there is any loose pollen. The stigma may then be dusted with pollen of another cultivar; transfer the pollen with a small watercolour paintbrush, or simply take an anther with your fingers or tweezers and brush it against the stigma surface. The stigma is at its most receptive when the surface is tacky. Always tag a crossed flower with a label as soon as you have done the pollination, because you could be doing several different crosses, and it will soon be difficult to remember which coupling was which. The convention is to write the name of the parent that bears the seed first (the seed parent) and the pollen parent second, so that a label might read 'Enchantment' × 'Red Carpet' where 'Enchantment' is the seed parent fertilized with pollen from 'Red Carpet'.

It may well be that the two parents you wish to cross are not in bloom at the same time. Nevertheless, it is easy to store pollen of the earlier kind. Anthers with loose pollen can be nipped off and placed in a plastic container, such as those used for rolls of photographic film. Remember to label the container clearly with the name of the lily. If anthers are removed just before they split to release their pollen, leave them in an open container in a dry, airy place, sealing them only when they have dried and have begun to release their pollen. Store containers in a refrigerator, where they can stay for several weeks or even months without the pollen losing viability. When the seed parent finally opens its flowers, the required pollen can be applied from the container using a small water-colour paintbrush.

A few weeks must pass before the successfully fertilized pods ripen and the seed can be harvested. Seedpods begin to turn beige and the tops split open. Then the seeds can be shelled out onto a piece of paper and the chaff gently blown away. If pods have not ripened on the plant by the time the autumn has reached its wintery end, cut off the seedheads and hang them somewhere dry and airy until the seed is ready to fall out. Place a sheet of paper below the hanging seedheads to gather any seeds that are released early.

There are so many avenues to explore in breeding that choosing a plan of action can be daunting. Newcomers might like to try the Asiatic hybrids first, because they set seed readily and the seeds grow quickly into bulbs of flowering size. The results are likely to be thoroughly enjoyable and rewarding. There is still a dearth of Asiatics with outward-facing flowers, and the pendent sorts are bewitching. Crossing very disparate types may not produce viable seed, crossing Asiatics with some of the Orientals is not likely to be successful, for example. Crossing within the groups or divisions should be relatively easy. Sometimes an apparently diverse liaison will give some viable seed. Hybridizing is always something of a gamble; long odds can occasionally provide a big winner.

A relatively open field for lily breeders is that of the

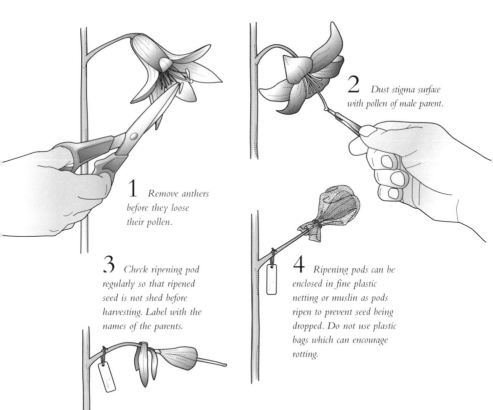

1 *Remove anthers before they loose their pollen.*

2 *Dust stigma surface with pollen of male parent.*

3 *Check ripening pod regularly so that ripened seed is not shed before harvesting. Label with the names of the parents.*

4 *Ripening pods can be enclosed in fine plastic netting or muslin as pods ripen to prevent seed being dropped. Do not use plastic bags which can encourage rotting.*

martagon-type hybrids, which are very popular with gardeners. Some good work is being done with these in Canada, but elsewhere they are almost ignored. Possibly this is because it takes them a few more years to achieve flowering, but if a little hybrid seed is sown each year, it is surprising how soon the years go by.

Many lily breeders are looking towards the increasing number of tetraploid lilies now available. These kinds hold double the usual number of chromosomes in each cell; with a few exceptions, those lilies found in the wild are diploid with 24 chromosomes, but there are occasional wild plants with three sets of chromsomes, triploids, with 36. The tetraploids have 48 chromosomes and on the whole they are more robust. Breeding with these may increase the diversity of the whole genus. Bulbs can be purchased of cultivars that have been artificially induced to give tetraploid forms. For example, 'Black Beauty' is widely sold as an infertile triploid, but there is now a tetraploid form that will set seed and has potent pollen.

Pests and other problems

A healthy start

Nearly every book about plants has its obligatory chapter on pests and diseases, very off-putting. Do not be disheartened by this one. All creation seems to have its problems and the lily is no exception, but, with relatively little care, threatening ones can usually be resolved easily.

It is a great help to start with healthy bulbs. As with all living things, healthy plants seem to ward off many ills. Slugs and some other subterranean organisms certainly prefer to attack through an open door, like a damaged organ. A healthy regime that embraces good drainage, with bulbs kept cool and moist, airy, sunlit spaces for the leaves and an adequate supply of nutrients will go a long way to ensure a trouble-free time.

Pests

Lilies are vulnerable to many pests, both the growing tops and the bulbs, so they can fall prey to hungry marauders. Lily enemy number one is the lily beetle. Larger opportunists are deer and rabbits. Slugs are always with us but the dangers these pests pose can be minimized.

Lily beetle

You cannot miss this pest. It has a black head and legs and the wing cases and thorax are uniform orange red. This handsome terrorist flies in to wreak havoc by eating foliage, copulating and laying eggs that hatch into larva, which are just as ravenously keen on the foliage as their parents. These creamy orange grubs are covered

'Masa' is a very strong Asiatic lily, often 2m (6ft) tall with large heads of bloom. Bulbs increase well and stems can be induced to give many bulbils in leaf axils.

56

with wet, black excrement to make them look like bird dirt, a mess which presumably protects them from adverse weather and from predators of which there seem precious few.

Lily beetles measure about 8mm (⅓in) long and 3mm (⅛in) wide, the larva are roughly 8mm (⅓in) long when fully grown. The first beetles can appear in early or mid-spring in most southern counties. They are very active up till midsummer and then, in my experience, become less active and numerous into the autumn.

Their distribution in Britain is expanding fast. Originally confined to the home counties, they have now been reported from most parts of the southern half of England though there remain unvisited pockets. There have been isolated reports of beetles further north in Lancashire and Yorkshire.

The lily's main enemy is the lily beetle, shown here with some of their less conspicuous larvae.

Spray plants with a systemic insecticide and with liquid derris. The regulations governing the use of chemicals are constantly changing, so the recommendation of a specific branded product is somewhat hazardous. Currently, one of the most effective of systemic insecticides to deter lily beetles is an aerosol spray containing imidacloprid and methiocarb. This formulation can also be bought as a powder to use as a soil drench for container-grown plants. Alternative contact insecticides use bifenthrin. The adult insects are more difficult to kill than the larvae.

Sprayers need not be elaborate or expensive. A handheld plastic one which holds 600ml (1 pint) is a simple, cheap and effective weapon. The larger ones holding 3 litres (5¼ pints) will take enough spray material to cover more extensive plantations. Most gardeners will not need huge quantities of spray at any one time and the dilution instructions on the packaging of the chemical may not be helpful for making small quantities. Where only a few plants need spraying it is best to use one of

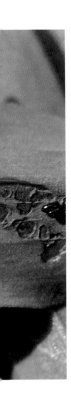

the ready-diluted bifenthrin products sold in hand-pump bottles, or use the aerosol mentioned above.

It is certainly wise to destroy any beetle sighted by catching it and squashing it. The same applies to the larva, but you may be able to avoid any larva developing. Normally the beetles are tricky to catch by hand as movement of the leaf precipitates a fall and the insects are next to impossible to find on the ground. They fall between debris or soil lumps and remain for a while upside down, only displaying their dark undersides, not their brilliant orange-red coats. A usual ploy is to lay a newspaper or cloth under the lily plants before trying to catch the beetles. However if plants are sprayed, the beetles take some poison, become more lethargic and are easier to catch. Try to make a daily run through the lilies from mid-spring onwards. If you cannot manage this it may be possible to inspire a friend or partner with a zest for the hunt.

Slugs

Slug control is helped by clean culture. Using slug pellets that are unattractive to birds or mammals is the most popular treatment. Metaldehyde in most pellets impedes the pests mobility and then causes them to exude huge quantities of slime. They become critically dehydrated so that they die unless rain follows quickly. The same chemical is also available as a liquid treatment. Some of the large slugs that look very impressive are not likely to be dangerous as they tend to restrict their activities to rotten material. It is the smaller slugs that are more pernicious. The dark garden slug and the paler brown field slug are the commonest and are eager vegetarians. They tend to remain below the soil surface or on the damp undersides of stones and thick vegetation during the day and emerge for nightly frolics. Their numbers fall if the ground is dug over and kept free of growth for a while. Trapping can also help and vegetable matter like citrus fruit peel is particularly appealing to them. Pieces of peel left out in the evening and collected early in the morning often provides a worthwhile catch. Jam jars or saucers pressed into the soil surface and half filled with stale beer will encourage a boozy excess, which will leave many slugs dead or incapable. By far the most important time to launch an onslaught on slugs is at the end of winter and the beginning of spring. This is a very active time for them. A slug allowed to reach summer can lay 200–300 eggs.

Vine Weevil

This pest became more of a problem as certain chemicals were removed from the market. They are normally more of a nuisance in pots than in the open garden. However, new proprietary treatments are now available and these are proving very satisfactory applied to potting compost. They will normally prevent trouble for the complete growing season.

It is the fat, creamy white grubs that cause the most damage, as they feed on the roots and sometimes parts of the bulb. They are a little more than 10mm (½in) long with light brown heads and rather arched bodies. The adult is a dull black beetle around 9mm (⅓in) long. Vine weevil larvae can be killed by watering pots with the insecticide imidacloprid marketed as a soil drench.

Wireworms

These are often numerous in newly cultivated grassland. They bore their tunnels through lily scales just as they do to potato tubers, but they are one of the less numerous of the garden pests. Millipedes can also attack lily bulbs, but their numbers are not usually huge, and they are often only a second-wave annoyance that comes along where there is damaged tissue. There is currently no effective insecticide available to amateur gardeners for controlling these pests. Wireworm numbers soon decline after the ground has been in cultivation for a couple of years.

The adult vine weevil eats lily leaves while their grubs destroy the roots and sometimes the bulbs.

Aphids

These can sometimes invade lilies, but they rarely build up huge numbers. However, a few can do a lot of harm by transmitting virus diseases. They should not be ignored, and they are easily dealt with by the systemic insecticides recommended for lily beetle or by other aphid-specific insecticides.

Rabbits, deer and moles

Only some gardeners are likely to be worried by deer and need to contemplate the considerable expense of deer-proof fencing, but rabbits are another matter. A local gamekeeper or pest control service will help you exterminate rabbits and when this is done, you should quickly enclose your whole garden with chicken wire to a height of 90cm (3ft) but with a vital 25cm (10in) below ground and a further 8cm (3in) at a right angle away from the garden. In my present garden this has proved very effective.

Moles cause trouble by burrowing below bulbs when searching for worms and other food. The person who discovers an easy and humane way to get rid of garden moles is sitting on a fortune. At present the only effective measure is the use of old-fashioned mole traps. When tripped, these kill instantly. Disregard all such nonsense as pushing holly twigs into the runs or planting caper spurges. The sap from these spurges was once thought to be a cure for facial moles; to think spurges are useful against the animal is a complete misunderstanding.

DISEASES

Viruses

These are by far the most important of lily diseases but need cause no very great dread. There are several viruses that can infect many plants including lilies, the most obvious and widespread being cucumber mosaic virus which causes pale streaks in the leaves and in heavy attacks, the leaves and flowers can be distorted and acquire a brittle texture. Tulip breaking virus produces a mottled effect. A peculiar disease is lily symptomless virus where plants have the appearance of general debility and are lacklustre in comparison to unaffected neighbours. Try not to diagnose this trouble when in fact you are looking at a plant that is suffering from overcrowding or from disturbance below, caused by animals such as moles.

There is no cure for virus and infected plants should be destroyed. Some lilies show symptoms more markedly than others. *L. longiflorum* and *L. candidum* are susceptible and soon lose a lot of their vigour and eventually die. *L. lancifolium* can carry virus with the leaf striping or mottling being rather understated and which only slowly affects the overall performance of the plants. Virus passed from such plants may have a more virulent effect on other lilies. The normal means of viral transfer is via the sap ingested by aphids, which then inject it into their next plant host. Cucumber mosaic virus is contagious and can be spread by handling diseased plants.

Fungus troubles

Botrytis elliptica, also known as lily disease, is common when the conditions are suitable. These conditions will be wet weather when plants are in a crowded airless situation. Attacks normally begin on the lower leaves. They develop brown, spreading blotches, look as if frosted and will lose their substance, collapse and wither. A very bad attack will clear all foliage and attack the stem but this is exceptional. Although such plants will be severely weakened they are rarely killed. There are no fungicides available to gardeners to cure this disease. Control can be helped by spraying Bordeaux mixture or benomyl early in the growing season. The fungus forms resting spores in dead leaves, so remove affected leaves promptly to avoid contaminating the soil.

Basal rot, *Fusarium oxysporum*, affects a variety of bulbs including lilies. Starting at the base, the affected area spreads until the bulb is destroyed. Starting with healthy bulbs and planting in soil that has not held diseased bulbs will make attacks unlikely. If bulbs have just begun to be affected, the dark brown, infected tissue can be cut away and the surfaces dusted with sulphur.

DRAINAGE

Healthy root systems are the basis for healthy plants. Energetic rooting is stimulated and maintained by an open root network with enough air in the soil to allow quick drainage of excess water. Conditions that are too wet will encourage slugs and snails, which nibble the bulbs and provide an open door for disease.

FROST

Low soil temperatures are rarely a problem on their own; it is the combination of cold and wet that can exacerbate any slight problem. A bruised or damaged area may start a serious rot, and this is likely to attract the attention of passing slugs.

Late frosts that come after lilies have begun to shoot through the ground can cause damage. Light damage will result in the young leaves losing their lively texture and collapsing. Bad damage will result in distorted stems or the death of all the above ground parts. This loss can kill the whole plant.

Late frosts of such intensity that plants could be destroyed are unlikely by the time most lilies have got around to emerging from the soil. *L. regale* is one that I find more likely to be damaged than most. Our practice is to cover emerging lilies with horticultural fleece when frosts are forecast. A pile of cut pieces is kept at the ready and when these are disposed over the plants this cover is almost always enough to defeat frost. Obviously those plants or clumps growing in more exposed places are the more vulnerable. Surrounding shrubs and other growing plants will shield nearby lilies.

Choosing
Your Lilies

There are a lot of lilies to choose from. Botanists list between 80 and 100 lilies in the wild, and there is a register, compiled by the Royal Horticultural Society, that lists thousands of garden hybrids; of these, several hundred are available, but some can take a bit of searching to find. The *RHS Plant Finder*, a book detailed in the next chapter, can be a great help in finding sources for those currently available, but there is a constant flow of new cultivars, often appearing in garden centres before they are listed in the *RHS Plant Finder*. Normally, you should expect those lilies on offer at garden centres and by bulb specialists to be reliable and worth trying. The illustrations used on packaged lilies are always a great help, and of these packaged kinds, the majority of Asiatic hybrids have upward-facing flowers. There are some cultivars with semi-double flowers, but I find these unpleasing as they destroy the clean lines of the orthodox lily. But that is simply a matter of personal preference.

The wild lilies

A restricted selection of lily species is listed below. The main criteria for selection are that they are available and reliable, two not unrelated characteristics. The demure *L. mackliniae* and the strange *L. nepalense* can be a little more demanding than the others in their cultivation requirements, but handled sensibly, they can give good results and they are certainly exciting in their individuality. The number that follows each species name indicates the group to which it belongs. Species are listed in the numerical order of these groups (see p.16).

'Pink Tiger' is a lively, wiry-stemmed Asiatic with pyramids of nodding blooms.

L. martagon (1) is a favourite with most gardeners. Once established, it can carry on for decades with little help. While it does well in light shade, its initial spot should not be threatened by encroaching shrubs or other strong plants. It will grow in many types of soils provided drainage is reasonable, although newly planted bulbs can sulk for a year; they may be rooting and declining to show growth above ground. Its clones vary a little in height, 1.2–2m (4–6ft) is normal. In early summer, the erect stems display their foliage in a number of well-separated whorls, and above these will be a narrow pyramid or cylinder of flowers. These are pendent, with the petals curling back and trying to touch their bases. Mauve-pink is the usual petal colour, but the depth of colour can vary from light to dark, and they are usually heavily freckled, but some are less so. Albino forms can be spotted or clear. Flowers open in early summer. Height:1–1.7m (3–5½ft).

L. pardalinum (2) is the leopard lily, a strong North American species sometimes represented by *L. pardalinum* var. *giganteum*, which is a particularly good erect form of natural hybrid origin. The bulbs are rhizomatous and look like a mat of scales with growing points around the edge. The leopard lilies can form impressive clumps over the years. The clean green stems have their leaves arranged in well-separated whorls, and the orange-red to crimson turk's-cap flowers are hung out at an angle, like lanterns on long stalks. Flower centres are golden and petals are marked by dark 'leopard' spots. It looks well standing in light woodland conditions or with shrubs. Flowers open in mid- to late summer. Height: 1–1.5m (3–5ft).

Lilium pardalinum. *The American group leopard lily blooms in midsummer, exciting colour allied to graceful habit. It is one of the easiest and most persistent of species.*

Lilium canadense.
*Most growers will
pick this as one of
the most graceful
of all lilies.*

L. canadense (2) is another North American species, but this one has stoloniferous bulbs, sending out stout stolons, 5–15cm (2–6in) long, from the parent bulb and producing new bulbs at the end of each stolon. Once established in open soil rich in organic matter, it can prove to be one of the most distinguished and elegant of all lilies. The foliage is whorled, and the widely spaced flowers hang looking downwards with their petals sweeping outwards and then gently upwards. Flower colour is usually a clear yellow with dark dots, but the wild population varies from pale yellow to red. It has been cultivated since the 1600s, but the fact that it is not widespread in gardens indicates an introverted nature. Success can be very sweet. Flowers open in midsummer. Height: 1.2–2m (4–6ft).

L. candidum (3) is the Madonna lily, a species cultivated since before the Christian era, both as a decorative plant and an edible bulb. It is usually thought of as a plant for cottage gardens, as it seems to flourish in the conditions you might expect to obtain in such places. It seems to enjoy neglect once the right position has been found; this should be a sunny site with well-drained soil. Unlike other lilies, the bulbs should be planted shallowly with their noses just below the surface. Good clumps can be obtained, even with the top half of the bulbs exposed. It is unusual in another respect: a rosette of leaves remains in winter to mark the bulb's position. The Madonna lily is also tolerant of alkaline soils. When planting, imagine that it will reach the size of a shrub and allow some room for spread over the years. Keep it well clear of any other lilies because it easily catches virus diseases carried by other plants, and these will cause steady or rapid deterioration of the plants. Suspect the worst if you see pale stripes in the leaves and some distortion; seek out and burn infected plants. Wide open, perfumed white flowers top the stems in early summer. Height: 1.2m (4ft).

Lilium pyrenaicum. A European of the Candidum group and probably the first of all lilies to bloom outside. An easy lily to grow once established.

L. pyrenaicum (3) is so precocious that it is often flowering in late spring. The very leafy stems carry several curled up, spotted pendent flowers, similar in form to the martagon lily but bright yellow and sometimes tinged with green. Petals are usually conspicuously marked with black dots. The aroma, if detected, is not pleasant. It is very hardy and has escaped into the wild in some places where it was originally introduced as a garden plant. Flowers open from late spring to midsummer. Height: 50–75cm (20–30in).

L. bulbiferum (3) is a species found in the mountains of southern Europe. It is the only European species to be involved in the breeding of the Asiatic hybrids. It grows strongly with stout stems that are well clothed with relatively broad, mid-green leaves below heads of wide, bowl-shaped, deep tangerine flowers marked with some dots. It can produce bulbils in the leaf axils, some clone more freely than others. Flowers open in late spring or early summer, making it one of the earlier species. Height: 75cm (30in).

Lilium bulbiferum.
A showy early flowering European of the Candidum group.

L. speciosum (4) is a Japanese species and is one of the latest to bloom, opening in early autumn with recurved, hanging flowers, which flood the air with scent. The wiry, slender stems have stalked, broad leaves, and the blooms are widely spaced. Flower colour varies: some are a wonderful pure white, others are flushed with pink, and some are more heavily painted with crimson-pink shades. The petal surfaces have raised points and are dotted with crimson. Alkaline soils are poisonous to these bulbs; where soils are limy, bulbs will have to be pot-grown. Flowers in pots open in late summer and early autumn. Height: 1–1.7m (3–5½ft).

L. auratum (4) is another Japanese species and also a lime-hater. It is quite exceptional when grown well, with strong, slender stems, broad foliage and wide-open flowers capable of a 25–30cm (10–12in) diameter. These are usually white with central golden stripes on each petal to give a star effect. There can be some small crimson spots and some individuals may have a crimson suffusion through the petals. It is usually grown as a container plant, where it needs a gritty, ericaceous potting compost and a well-ventilated environment. It can be splendid in such an environment, performing best in large containers where it can be top-dressed periodically with leafmould or similar organic matter. It is not grown so widely now that we have so many of their stronger hybrid offspring to choose from. Flowers open in late summer with strong perfume. Height: 0.75–2.2m (2½–7ft).

Lilium henryi. *Distinct member of the Asian group and one of the toughest of all lilies. It it unusual in that it is not only tolerant of lime but actually seems to enjoy it.*

L. henryi (5) is an important and very hardy, long-lived species, which will grow in any garden soil, even one that is rich in lime (alkaline). Left to its own devices, it produces strong stems at sloping angles with quite large, mid-orange flowers. The petals curl back and display the papillae, a series of raised points crowded on the surface, especially on the inner half, of each petal. The flower colour fades a bit with age, but the plants do not flag in vigour; they get more numerous and floriferous as the seasons pass. It is this species that has been crossed with Trumpet hybrids and more recently with Oriental hybrids to provide new races of lime-tolerant garden lilies. Flowers open in early to mid-summer. Height: 1–3m (3-10ft), but usually with stems at a slanting angle.

L. lancifolium (5) is the tiger lily, still better known to many as *L. tigrinum*. It is a splendid plant growing strongly with almost black stems and dark, narrow leaves below heads of nodding, rich orange flowers heavily marked with dark spots. The petals recurve backwards. A stem may produce up to 100 or more bulbils in the leaf axils, so propagation is no problem. The bulbils grow strongly and make flowering plants in two years. It is such a strong grower that it can be infected with a virus and lose only a little strength. Unfortunately, this means that it can grow happily while also being a source of virus infection for other lilies. Clean plants soon make a fine stand

Lilium lancifolium. *This Asian group member is the tiger lily, known for many decades as* L. tigrinum.

and look well, but because of the possibility of carrying a virus they are best planted as far away from their relatives as possible. Flowers open in midsummer. Height: 1.5–2m (5–6ft).

L. mackliniae (5) is one of a group of lilies that look very similar to the closely related *Nomocharis* genus. Certainly, it is not what is envisaged as an orthodox lily. It has a refined, dainty performance. Narrow, rich green leaves are held more or less at right angles to the stem in a spiral arrangement. The blooms start to open in early to midsummer, one or two on the stems of young plants and perhaps six to a full dozen or more on those of really strong, established plants. The flowers are nodding caps, in the form of a globe, with only the very tips of the petals recurved. Outside petal surfaces are very much darker than the inner ones, which are white and just lightly flushed with a mauve-pink. The outer pigment can be a rich purple-rose concentrated at the stalk end and paling towards the petal tips; colour depth varies from plant to plant. This is a species that enjoys soil rich in organic matter, and in the British Isles, it grows better in the cooler conditions of northern England and Scotland than in the south. If tried in drier, warmer areas, try to moderate the harsher limits of these factors. Always look out for signs of virus infection: attacked plants quickly lose their vitality, and for this reason, make sure that newly obtained

bulbs are free of any leaf-mottling symptoms, and plant them away from other lilies that could be a source of infection. Plants raised from seed will, of course, start virus-free. Flowers open from early to late summer. Height: 12–75cm (4¾–30in), depending on the clone and growing conditions.

L. nepalense (5) was once a rarity, but many bulb dealers and nurserymen now offer it for sale. The stoloniform bulbs produce stems that can wander extensively before making themselves known above ground. Grown in pots, I have found them trying to escape through the drainage holes, so it may well be best to plant it in the garden having arranged a well-worked, open soil rich in organic matter. Flowering stems will carry one or more large, inflated, nodding trumpet flowers,

Lilium regale *'Album' is a Trumpet group lily that has the same heavily scented flowers as* Lilium regale *but without the dark buds that give the three outer petals their maroon outer sides.*

usually of lacquered lime-yellow, but the colour is dominated by the very dark maroon base, a staining that can encroach over two-thirds of each petal. It certainly is distinctive. Flowers usually open in late summer. Height: 25–75cm (10–30in).

L. regale (6) has been grown in gardens for a hundred years and has proved to be one of the most successful of the wild kinds. It grows quickly from seed and forms substantial bulbs which can last for many years. Growth starts early, too early sometimes as frost may still be about and can damage the shoots. The strong stems are clothed with dark narrow leaves, and in midsummer, the maroon-stained buds open to reveal large, white trumpets with honey-gold bases. Established bulbs can be very floriferous with 10–30 blooms, overflowing with perfume. It can be very good in large containers like half tubs. There is a pure white form, *L. regale* 'Album'. Flowers open in midsummer. Height: 0.6–2m (2–6ft), depending on age and site.

Lilium nepalense *is a very distinctive, quite dwarf species with large blooms and wandering subterranean stems, along which new bulbs can form.*

L. formosanum var. *pricei* (6) is a comic dwarf, a small variety of a species found in Taiwan. Disproportionately huge trumpet flowers top the short stems. The narrow throat of the flower expands widely at the mouth, all shining white. It grows easily from seed. Flowers open in mid- to late summer. Height: 15–25cm (6–10in).

L. longiflorum (6) is the Easter lily, which is grown widely under glass as a cut flower. In cool climates, it may be a touch tender to frost outside, but in other parts of the world it is grown in quantity in fields. It has a remarkable metabolism: seeds sown around late winter can result in flowering stems before the year's end. Freshly raised stock is a good idea as it is very vulnerable to virus. The buds and the large trumpet flowers are pure white and heavily fragrant. It does well in cool conservatories or greenhouses. *L. longiflorum* 'White American' is similar but with slightly shorter flowers. Outdoors, flowers of *L. longiflorum* usually bloom in late summer. Height: 30–100cm (12–39in), depending on bulb size and situation.

THE GARDEN LILIES

As with the wild lily species described above, the selection of cultivars in this section is based primarily on their availability

'Red Carpet' is one of the earliest Asiatics to bloom.

and reliabilty. The lilies are listed according to their classification, full details of which are given on pages 18–19.

DIVISION I: ASIATIC HYBRIDS

These lilies have concentric bulbs and scattered foliage. They are very easy in both containers and in the open garden. They tolerate a little lime in the soil, but like all lilies, they enjoy soils rich in organic matter. Asiatic lilies are divided into three groups by flower pose; by far the most numerous are the upward-facing types, but the outward-facing and pendent kinds should not be ignored. Flowers bloom from early to midsummer unless otherwise stated. Assume a normal height of around 75cm (30in) for first-year bulbs, with growth reaching up to 30cm (12in) taller the following year – any exceptions are noted.

DIVISION IA: ASIATIC HYBRIDS WITH UPWARD-FACING FLOWERS

Red- and orange-flowered cultivars

'Enchantment' is one of the most famous and successful of lilies. Introduced halfway through the last century, it quickly established itself as a leading garden plant and forged a dominant role in the cut flower market. The crowded flowerheads of wide, starry blooms are a fluorescent orange with a light dusting of tiny dark spots towards the centres. It is sturdy and easy to grow; bulbs increase quickly with many bulbils being produced by non-flowering or decapitated stems, although flowering stems will often also bear bulbils.

'Festival' is tricky to classify by the colour of the flowers, as these are a medley of gold, tan and orange with buds of maroon or chocolate brown. The pointed red petal tips give way to golden yellow before a central star of deep red, and the petals are seriously freckled with dark brown. It is a strong, upright plant with nearly black stems and narrow, dark green leaves below pyramid-shaped flowerheads, each made up of a generous number of tastefully spaced blooms. Altogether, it has a distinguished character. The flowers are slightly later to open, and it is perhaps up to 30cm (12in) taller than average Asiatic hybrids.

'**Firecracker**' is a very free-flowering cultivar, blooming in early and midsummer with shining, rich cherry red flowers. It reaches 1–1.2m (3–4ft) tall. (Illustrated on front cover.)

'**Red Carpet**' has uniformly rich orange-red, bowl-shaped flowers with wide petals. It usually begins to flower at the onset of early summer, June. It is a sturdy plant, rarely higher than 45cm (18in), but a bulb that increases steadily.

Yellow-flowered cultivars

'**Connecticut King**' is another established favourite used in huge quantities as a cut flower. The leaves are a fresh green, the stems are strong and the sizeable blooms of uniform golden yellow, free of spots.

'**Grand Cru**' has bold, wide-petalled, golden, bowl-shaped

'Grand Cru', a bicolour Asiatic with bold large heads in showy colours.

Yellow Blaze Group is usually the last of the Asiatics to come into bloom. Noticeable in the garden with tall stems and persistent good heads from bulbs that increase quickly.

flowers with the centres painted dark maroon. This is a bold, almost gaudy bit of contrast.

'Luxor' is a robust lily with an enviable rate of bulb increase. The large flowers are full yellow with a warmer flush of incipient tangerine towards the petal centres.

'Medaillon' has bowl-shaped flowers with broad, smooth petals of creamy yellow merging to gold in the centres. It is not too tall.

Yellow Blaze Group is distinguished by its vigorous, tallish growth, up to 1.2m (4ft), and by flowering late, often not opening until after midsummer and overlapping into autumn. The flowers are bright yellow with recurved petals boldly freckled and with gaps at the petal bases.

White- and pale-flowered cultivars

'Apollo' has smooth, milk-white blooms with a touch of pale, creamy yellow towards the centres. It is not tall.

'Sterling Star', an Asiatic which has had a long career as a cut flower and which is still a most pleasing pot and garden plant.

'Mont Blanc' has dark foliage and good-sized flowers of creamy white, which open from pleasing pink buds. It is not a novelty, but still a telling flower.

'Roma' is taller than most, sometimes reaching 1.5–2m (5–6ft) high when established. The flat, wide cream flowers have a light sprinkle of tiny dots as a ring around the throats. It is stately and gives good seedlings. Flowers later than many.

'Sterling Star' has pointed, white petals with dark spots. The flowerheads are wide and relatively tall. The leaves are narrow.

Pink-flowered cultivars

'Corina' has broad petals making even flowers of uniform rich pink-red with a few dark brown spots in the centres. It can reach 1–1.2m (3–4ft).

'Côte d'Azur' has sturdy stems with rosy pink flowers in full heads, reaching 45–60cm (18–24in). It has given some nice seedlings.

'**Montreux**' is a free-flowering, strong plant with many spreading blooms of full pink and an undertone of peach.

'**Rosita**' has a lilac tinge to the pink flowers; the initial stronger pink fades somewhat with age. The flower centres have some black spots. It stands about 75cm (30in) tall and has given some attractive seedlings.

'**Sorbet**' is an appealing cultivar with rich pink petal points that give way to white centres, which are peppered with magenta dots.

'**Vogue**' has uniform, soft pink, widely star-shaped flowers with pointed petals. It has a cool-looking personality.

Dwarf cultivars with upward-facing flowers

Breeders have realized the importance of the lily as a container plant. They are marketed as plants in bud or as bulbs, and it is possible to plan containers of lilies so that they give a variety of

'Sorbet' is one of a series of bicolour Asiatics, this one being a particularly fresh, bright lily that increases quickly.

colours and a succession of blooms. The Pixie Series contains many different colour clones, and 'Butter Pixie', 'Peach Pixie', 'Crimson Pixie' and 'White Pixie' are some examples. They are all dwarf, but some will go up to a daring 40cm (16in). They bloom early and make ideal container plants. There are other dwarf Asiatic hybrids, some marketed as a series in the same way as the Pixies, and some marketed under their individual names.

'Blackbird' is a squat lily with plenty of long, rich green leaves to back the heads of very deep red, open, star-shaped flowers.

'Country Life' is taller at 45cm (18in), but is still a first-class lily for the patio or at the front of a garden border. It has narrow, dark foliage and pointed, star-shaped flowers of a glowing deep yellow.

'Disco' is a similar height to 'Country Life' but has vibrant deep pink flowers.

'Orange Pixie' is one of the best – a real dwarf at around 20cm (8in) tall. Like all the Pixies, this is an attractive, well-behaved plant, and it has good heads of relatively large flowers in glowing uniform orange, which light up its station for a few weeks.

'Denia' is sometimes marketed as 'Denia Pixie'. It is an Asiatic dwarf with much freckled pink blooms.

LA hybrids

These were bred from the mating of *L. longiflorum* with various Asiatic hybrids (hence the title, LA). They are very vigorous plants with a generous attitude to propagation. Most of those introduced so far have upward-facing flowers with large, wide, bowl- or star-shaped blooms in massive flowerheads held on strong stems. All LA hybrids can be planted in expectation of impressive, bold effects. Some have a light perfume, but none of the present introductions have the heavy fragrance of the parent *L. longiflorum*. They are at their best through midsummer. They usually measure 1–1.2m (3–4ft) tall.

'**Fiery Fred**' is an extraordinarily vigorous LA hybrid growing up to 2m (6ft) tall. The pointed petals form wide and starry, bowl-shaped flowers of glowing deep orange, somewhat more golden in their centres. Each stem can bear well over 30 of the large blooms.

'**Moonshine**' is a very pleasant LA hybrid with the typical shining foliage. The green buds open to wide, pale lemon flowers, which fade in a few days to nearly pure white, the dark anthers adding a contrasting touch.

'**Rodeo**' is a sturdy kind, usually not more than 75cm (30in) tall. The rosy pink flowers with paler centres are carried in rather crowded heads.

'**Royal River**' is one of the most striking of a number of cultivars with rich pink flowers. These are large and an intense, deep maroon-pink.

DIVISION IB: ASIATIC HYBRIDS WITH OUTWARD-FACING FLOWERS

'**Fire King**' was introduced in the early 1930s and is still going very strong. It sends up stems about 1.2m (4ft) tall with a packed pyramid of wide, bowl-shaped flowers in deep, shining orange. It grows rapidly and opens early, perhaps the earliest of all the Asiatic hybrids.

'**King Pete**' is a large-flowered lily with rather flat, lightly dotted, creamy yellow blooms with richer, almost tangerine, centres.

Division Ic: Asiatic hybrids with pendent flowers

Citronella Group was introduced in the 1950s and has been highly regarded by gardeners ever since. The flowers open in midsummer, a little later than most Asiatic hybrids, and then remain in bloom for an extended season as flowers appear in succession. Marketed bulbs may be of one or several clones, and these can differ, especially in flower size. What remains constant is the pleasing, pendent pose and the bright glowing yellow of the flowers with recurved petals that flaunt their black beauty spots. Clones with large flowers will have fewer of them than the very floriferous smaller flowered clones. All are wonderful and very effective, particularly between shrubs or as a focal point in a border. Heights vary from 1–2m (3–6ft).

'**Pink Panther**' has upright stems that carry pyramids of well-displayed blooms with recurved petals in pleasing pastel shades of peachy pink sprinkled with dots. They grow to 75–100cm (30–39in) tall.

'**White Tiger**' has neat, upright growth with narrow, dark leaves and nodding, wide, white blooms. The petals gently sweep out and back, and the white is made the more effective by the addition of some tiny dark dots and a greenish hint in the flower centres.

North hybrids inherit their pendent pose and heads of widely spaced, recurved flowers from *L. lankongense*. The flowers are mostly in cream, pink or peach shades with more-or-less dark spotting. They stand around 1–1.5m (3–5ft) tall and love an open soil that is rich in organic matter. They are named after members of the North family. 'Barbara North' is a graceful cultivar with narrow foliage and pendent, rich pink flowers with recurved petals.

DIVISION II: MARTAGON-TYPE HYBRIDS

L. × *dalhansonii* 'Marhan' was introduced in 1891 and remains an outstanding garden cultivar. It is the result of *L. martagon* var. *album* crossed with *L. hansonii*. Any other plants bred between these two species can also be relied on to give excellent service. *L. hansonii* is similar in appearance to *L. martagon*, but the petals do not curl up so much and the flower colour is golden orange with spots and a thicker texture – the likeness to bits of marmalade comes to mind. In appearance, 'Marhan' is clearly an intermediate of the two species. It has pendent, tawny orange flowers, much decorated with darker spots. The bulbs increase steadily and if given a place to colonize, you are looking at a lease of between one or two decades. Flowers open in early summer. Height: 1.4–2m (4½–6ft), depending on the site and the age of the plants.

DIVISION IV: AMERICAN HYBRIDS

'Cherrywood' is a hybrid raised by Derek Fox in Essex. It is one of the relatively few hybrids of the American species group.

'Cherrywood' is one of relatively few hybrids arising from the mating of North American species. You can see the influence of the seed parent, *L. pardalinum*, in the erect stems, the few whorls of foliage and the nodding pose of widely spaced flowers. The colour is also rather similar: rich red petal tips marked with decorative, dark spots give way to tangerine

gold centres. The flowers are made more elegant than most by the petals, which swing wide in an arc, but do not try to 'touch their toes' like those of the parent. The bulbs are of a similar rhizomatous type to the parent and need to be carefully lifted and propagated. Flowers open from midsummer and last for several weeks, at which time they make a telling, elegant picture. Height: up to 2m (6ft).

DIVISION VI: TRUMPET HYBRIDS

They are strong growers and all have that important lily perfume. The bulbs are concentric, usually with pointed noses, and these grow well in both containers and the open garden; plant each bulb no closer than 30cm (12in) apart if they are to be left for more than one season. Trumpet hybrids enjoy well-worked soil incorporating plenty of organic matter and will go from strength to strength, splendid the first year but better the next, with taller stems and larger flowerheads. They can often

Pink Perfection Group flowers are very impressive, hugely perfumed and usually a very dark colour.

be left for three to five years, but then need lifting and a thorough job done of their division. The foliage is usually narrow, plentiful and scattered along the stems. The flowers may open in early summer but are usually at their best during mid- to late summer. Traditionally, Trumpet hybrids of Division VIa, with trumpet-shaped flowers, are the 'proper' lilies, in that they typify the popular image of the plant. In the list below, the sub-divisions are given after the name of each plant.

African Queen Group lilies have large heads of shining orange and tan trumpets spilling over with heady perfume.

African Queen Group (Division VIa) are really robust plants with large, trumpet-shaped flowers of glowing rich tangerine. They reach up to 1.2–2m (4–6ft) tall. The breeding of golden-flowered Trumpet hybrids led to some in which the pigmentation was concentrated to give orange flowers. These were bred further, and African Queen Group is one outstanding group of clones that was eventually picked.

Golden Splendor Group (Division VIa) has tanned buds that open to reveal glowing golden, trumpet-shaped flowers. Height is normally around 1.2m (4ft). *L. regale* 'Royal Gold' is usually billed as 'the golden *regale*' – a just description as it is strong with dark maroon buds, and it can have magnificent, many-headed stems of rich golden flowers. Although listed as a cultivar, there are certainly at least two clones marketed under this name, though they are very close in appearance.

Pink Perfection Group (Division VIa) once included clones that varied in colour from pale to very dark pinks. Now it is the dark ones that are marketed, with large, trumpet-shaped flowers of a deep pink that has hints of maroon in its make-up, but it is probably best described unromantically as beetroot-pink. Height can be well in excess of 2m (6ft), but usually less in the first year.

'Bright Star' (Division VIc) is one of the results of intercrossing *L. henryi* with Trumpet species like *L. centifolium*, something done on a very large scale by Jan de Graaff in 1938. Huge numbers of his seedlings were raised and sorted into various categories when they bloomed. Some were close to Trumpets in form, but there were others with flat flowers, and these were termed Sunburst types. 'Bright Star' was typical of these, and the stance follows that of *L. henryi* with strong, sloping stems and broad leaves, but the flowers are wide with recurved petal tips. They are white with throats a dark honey shade that advances up the centre of each petal to give a star shape; this star is itself centred by a smaller green one formed by the nectary furrows. It is a persistent plant and can look well grouped between shrubs. Flowers open from late summer to early autumn, and the sloping stems reach 1–1.2m (3–4ft) long

Division VII: Oriental hybrids

Initially, these hybrids were bred by intercrossing forms of *L. speciosum* and *L. auratum*. The results were dramatic. The offspring made stronger plants than either of the parents, but their spectacular flowers, looks and perfume were inherited. They inherited the morbid distaste for lime, however, but see 'Black Beauty' for the latest developments in this field. Oriental hybrids make excellent container plants, and they are good in gardens with lime-free or acid soils. The bulbs are widely concentric, and the leaves are alternate or scattered along the stems and usually with stalks. Flowers usually bowl-shaped.

*'Journey's End' is
a fine Oriental
cultivar, closer to
Lilium speciosum
than many in looks
and in its late
blooming habit.*

'**Acapulco**' has opulent, wide-open flowers in glowing, uniform deep pink with a few small red dots. The flowers are made to look even larger by the pointing petals and have the expected intoxicating scent. Flowers open mid- to late summer. Height: 75cm (30in).

'**Black Beauty**' is the first to be marketed of a new race of hybrids called Orienpets (see p.21). It contains some blood from *L. henryi*, the lime-loving species, and as a result, this cultivar is found to tolerate some lime in the soil. The bulbs can be prodigiously strong, and the stems are mighty enough to carry big loads of flowers: 50 per head is common, 100 per head is not too exceptional, and a 150 per head a possibility. The individual flowers hanging from the wide stems are dark crimson-pink with narrow, white petal margins and a white-outlined green star in their centres. Petals sweep outwards and are then strongly recurved, which lends emphasis to the dark, protruding anthers. It can be safely recommended as a garden plant. Flowers open from late summer to early autumn. Height: 1.2–2m (4–6ft).

'**Casa Blanca**' is now an established favourite in gardens. It has very large, more-or-less outward-facing flowers, easily capable of 20cm (8in) in diameter, all snow–white except for a greenish tinge that may be present towards the centre. Flowers open from mid- to late summer. Height: 1–1.4m (3–4½ft).

'Casa Blanca' is a fine Oriental with very large, wide, scented flowers of snowy whiteness.

'Journey's End' is a late-flowering hybrid, and is closer in breeding and appearance to the late-flowering *L. speciosum*. It has wider, flatter flowers than the species, but the petal tips are gently recurved. They are crimson, shading to narrow margins of white. The flowers are well spaced and can be numerous on the stems of established plants. Flowers open from late summer to early autumn. Height: to 2m (6ft).

'Mona Lisa' is a dwarf type with large, upward- or outward-facing rosy pink blooms broadly edged with white. It is most useful in containers. Flowers open from mid- to late summer. Height: 35–50cm (15–20in).

'Star Gazer' was made famous as a cut flower and was the first of the Oriental hybrids to bear upward-facing flowers and an easy constitution. Even very small bulbs give good results, and it is a fine container or open-garden plant. The deep crimson petals are thinly margined with white, while the centres are marked with even deeper crimson spots. Flowers open from mid- to late summer. Height: 1.5m (5ft) from well-established bulbs, but perhaps only half this height from small, young bulbs.

FURTHER INFORMATION

There are fairly frequent articles in the gardening press about lilies, and they are not entirely ignored by television programmes, but on the whole such coverage runs over well-worn tracks. For more detailed and wider information you may have to go a little further. All postal addresses and telephone numbers mentioned are within the United Kingdom and correct at the time of going to press.

AWARDS

The following lilies have received the RHS Award of Garden Merit (AGM):

African Queen Group
'Apollo'
'Casa Blanca'
'Fata Morgana'
'Garden Party'
Golden Splendor Group
'Grand Cru'
'Joy'
'King Pete'
'Lennox'
L. candidum
L. henryi

L. lancifolium var. *splendens*
L. martagon
L. martagon var. *album*
L. pardalinum var. *giganteum*
L. pumilum
L. regale
L. × *testaceum*
'Medaillon'
'Novo Centro'
Pink Perfection Group
'Sam'

BOOKS

The Gardener's Guide to Growing Lilies, M. Jefferson-Brown (David & Charles, 1995). Covers most aspects of lily culture, the botany, the species and the hybrids.

Lilies, Edward A. McRae (Timber Press, 1998). Particularly good reviewing of the history of breeding, in which the author himself was involved.

Growing Lilies, Derek Fox (Christopher Helm, 1985). Quite comprehensive and especially good on the species.

Lilies of the World, H.B.D. Woodcock and W.T. Stearn (Country Life, 1950). Remains an excellent reference book for all the species known at the time. Little about hybrids.

Lilies and Related Plants (see 'RHS Lily Group' below)

RHS LILY GROUP

There is no specialist lily society in Britain, possibly because the work of the RHS Lily Group provides much of what is needed. They arrange the publication of an annual illustrated paperback booklet, called *Lilies and Related Plants*, which makes interesting reading and keeps one abreast of what is happening with lilies. Most members of the group will consider their modest membership fee very amply repaid by the free annual seed list to which members here and abroad contribute. A newsletter is sent out periodically, normally at least three times a year. There is also an annual auction of bulbs to help raise funds. The group is advertising itself at some of the major shows and usually arranges a display at one of the RHS summer shows. They also organize conferences and garden visits, sometimes taking the form of a three day outing to a particular part of the country. There is also a regularly updated website at **www.rhslilygroup.org**.

PLACES TO VISIT

Lilies will be seen at all the major shows and some will be grown by the various botanical gardens. Other important gardens are likely to have some lilies, but their collections will vary over the years. Plans are going ahead to establish National Collections of species lilies. These are likely to be housed in two English Heritage gardens and a Scottish National Trust garden.

The RHS Gardens at Wisley usually have a good number of lilies growing during the summer months. Other gardens with RHS connections are likely to prove useful hunting grounds, including Harlow Carr outside Harrogate. Some members of the Lily Group open their private gardens, and these are obviously gardens to be targeted. As lilies bloom at the peak months for garden visiting, it is likely that many of those gardens open under the National Gardens Scheme will have some in their displays.

WEBSITES

Information about lilies will be found on the RHS website, especially in the advice sections. Start with **www.rhs.org.uk** – headings listed are events, gardens, plants, advice, science, education, publications, join us, and shopping. Advice is updated so that it is applicable to the time of year. Lily beetle features on this during the growing months.

The RHS Lily Group's website is **www.rhslilygroup.org**. Headings listed are: programme, plant topic, news, membership, and links. By printing each new plant topic as the site is updated, a very useful reference source can be built up, sometimes with bits of information not readily available elsewhere.

North American lily enthusiasts will be the first to check the wide-ranging site at: **pine.usask.ca/cofa/departments/hort/ hortinfo/misc/**. This has a very long list of topic headings, including lilies. I have found the information here likely to be of interest to British growers as well as those across the Atlantic.

SEED SUPPLIERS

As many lily species are scarce as bulbs, raising seeds may be the only way to acquire many rarer kinds. A splendid selection of species and hybrid seeds is contained in the annual seed list of the RHS Lily Group. The Alpine Garden Society also have a fascinating annual list and this often contains the smaller species lilies, but not exclusively. The RHS also has an annual seed list, which is free on request. This is likely to contain lilies.

Of the commercial sources, the most outstanding list is that of Chiltern Seeds, Bortree Stile, Ulverstone, Cumbria LA12 7PB. This contains many species, and is especially rich in North American kinds. It also has seeds of various hybrid strains, including some from New Zealand.

BULB SUPPLIERS

Garden centres offer bulbs in autumn and spring. They may be displayed loose in crates backed by an illustration, or in plastic bags of one or three bulbs with an attached illustration. All of these are usually very good value, but you need to make sure that you are not buying old, dried-out stock or bulbs with a growing shoot trying to escape the bag.

Use of the *RHS Plant Finder* book or CD-ROM will be helpful in locating nurseries that offer specific kinds of lily bulbs. Some of the main suppliers are listed here:

Avon Bulbs, Burnt House Farm, Mid-Lambrook, South Petherton, Somerset TA13 5HE. Not a long list. Some species are offered for autumn delivery and others for spring delivery; the latter include one or two not usually available elsewhere.

Bloms Bulbs Ltd, Primrose Nurseries, Melchbourne, Bedfordshire MK44 1ZZ. A range of better-known species, sometimes with one or two rarer types. A selection of cultivars of the main divisions, with a wider choice than most of the dwarf kinds recommended for container culture.

Burncoose and South Down Nurseries, Gwennap, Redruth, Cornwall TR16 6BJ. Lists quite a lot of both species and hybrids, including a number of cultivars not found elsewhere.

de Jager and Sons Ltd, Staplehurst Road, Marden, Kent TN12 9BP. Covers species and hybrids in wider variety than many, usually with several of the rarer species, and a wide selection of Oriental hybrids with other main types.

Jacques Amand Ltd, The Nurseries, 145 Clamp Hill, Stanmore, Middlesex HA7 3JS. A wide selection of species and hybrids, some not found elsewhere.

Paul Christian, PO Box 468, Wrexham, Clwyd LL13 9XR. Website: www.rareplants.co.uk. Only species offered, but the list includes some rare and newly introduced kinds

R.V. Roger Ltd, The Nurseries, Pickering, North Yorkshire YO18 7HG. Offer both species and hybrids in reasonable variety.

van Tubergen UK Ltd, Bressingham, Diss, Norfolk IP22 2AB. Offer both species and hybrids.

FALSE LILIES

The word lily has been used loosely in the past to mean flowers, often bulbous ones. Understandably, this has caused quite a bit of confusion. The following list includes some so-called 'lilies', but here they own up to their proper botanical name. The common name is given first, followed by the latin name, and finally the family name. A glance down the list shows that only one even belongs the lily family, Liliaceae.

African corn lily (*Ixia*) Iridaceae
African lily (*Agapanthus*) Alliaceae
Arum lily (*Zantedeschia*) Araceae
Belladonna lily (*Amaryllis belladonna*) Amaryllidaceae
Bluebead lily (*Clintonia borealis*) Convallariaceae
Bugle lily (*Watsonia*) Iridaceae
Daylily (*Hemerocallis*) Hemerocallidaceae
Glory lily (*Gloriosa*) Colchicaceae
Guernsey lily (*Nerine sarniensis*) Amaryllidaceae
Kaffir lily (*Schizostylis*) Iridaceae
Lily-of-the-valley (*Convallaria*) Convallariaceae
Lily Pink (*Aphyllanthes*) Aphyllanthaceae
Peruvian lily (*Alstroemeria*) Alstromeriaceae
Plantain lily (*Hosta*) Hostaceae
St Bernard's lily (*Anthericum liliago*) Anthericaceae
St Bruno's lily (*Paradisea liliastrum*) Asphodelaceae
Scarborough lily (*Cyrtanthus elatus*) Amaryllidaceae
Toad lily (*Tricyrtis*) Convallariaceae
Torch lily (*Kniphofia*) Asphodelaceae
Trout lily (*Erythronium*) Liliaceae
Voodoo lily (*Sauromatum venosum*) Araceae
Water lily (*Nuphar* and *Nymphae*) Nymphaeaceae
Wood lily (*Trillium*) Trilliaceae

INDEX

Page numbers in **bold** refer
to illustrations

Acknowledgements

Illustrations: Patrick Mulrey
Copy-editor: Simon Maughan
RHS Editor: Barbara Haynes
Proofreader: Rae Spencer-Jones
Index: Dorothy Frame

The Publisher would like to thank
the following people for their kind
permission to reproduce their
photographs:
The Garden Picture Library: 3 (Steven
Wooster), 7 (John Glover), 15 (J. S. Sira),
65 (Chris Burrows), 67 (Christopher
Fairweather), 68 (Lamontagne),
70 (Mark Bolton), 71 (Chris Burrows),
72 (Sunniva Harte), 73 (Howard Rice),
76 (J. S. Sira), 78 (Mayer/Le Scanff),
80 (John Glover), 84 (Mark Bolton),
87 (Chris Burrows)
Garden Matters: 58
Michael Jefferson-Brown: 8, 20, 21, 23,
24, 27, 29, 30, 33, 34, 37, 39, 40, 42, 45,
57, 66, 69, 74, 77. 79, 83, 85, 88
Ed Sheppard: 60

Jacket Image: The Garden Picture
Library (Brian Carter)

	DATE DUE		

Wharton and the Illustrated Travel Book," paper delivered at the meeting of the American Literature Association in Baltimore, May 1995, for drawing my attention to Edith Wharton's concern with illustrations for her texts.

64. Wharton, *Backward Glance*, 378.

65. Ibid., 209.

66. Robert Scholes, *Structuralism in Literature: An Introduction* (New Haven: Yale Univ. Press, 1974), 130.

67. Yaeger, *Honey-Mad Women*.

CODA

1. Benstock, *No Gifts from Chance*, 311.

2. For full biographical information on Wharton's war efforts see R. W. B. Lewis, *Edith Wharton: A Biography* (New York: Harper & Row, 1975), 363–403; Benstock, *No Gifts from Chance*, 301–49; and Alan Price, *The End of Innocence: Edith Wharton and the First World War* (New York: St. Martin's, 1996).

3. In "Narrative Practices and Construction of Identity: Edith Wharton" (*Commonwealth and American Women's Discourse: Essays in Criticism*, 278–91), Radhika Mohanram argues that because Wharton was "other" in America because she was an artist, and "other" in Europe because she was a colonial, she constructed in her letters and her autobiography, as well as in her fiction, a spiral of identities. She was always the *sujet-en-procès*.

4. Wharton, *Backward Glance*, 352.

5. The articles that became *Fighting France* appeared as "In Argonne," *Scribner's Magazine* 57 (June 1915): 651–60; "In Lorraine and the Vosges," *Scribner's Magazine* 58 (October 1915): 430–42; and "In the North," *Scribner's Magazine* 58 (November 1915): 600–610. Wharton calls *Fighting France* a "little book" and "scribbles" in *A Backward Glance*, 339, 352–53.

6. Wright, *Edith Wharton Abroad*, 36.

7. Wharton, *A Motor-Flight Through France*, 160.

8. For Wharton's own account of this, see *A Backward Glance*, 345–57.

9. For a full discussion of the characteristics and evocations of *Motor-Flight*, see my "Edith Wharton and Travel Writing as Self-Discovery," 257–67.

10. See MacCannell, *The Tourist*, x.

Index